W9-BRM-949

TAKING HOLD OF TORAH

THE HELEN AND MARTIN SCHWARTZ
LECTURES IN JEWISH STUDIES,
1996

Sponsored by the
Robert A. and Sandra S. Borns
Jewish Studies Program,
Indiana University

TAKING
HOLD
OF
TORAH

JEWISH COMMITMENT
AND COMMUNITY
IN AMERICA

Arnold M. Eisen

INDIANA UNIVERSITY PRESS

Bloomington • Indianapolis

The paper used in this publication meets the minimum requirements of American National Standard for Information Sciences—Permanence of Paper for Printed Library Materials, ANSI Z39.48–1984.

Manufactured in the United States of America

Library of Congress Cataloging-in Publication Data

Eisen, Arnold M., date
Taking hold of Torah : Jewish commitment and community
in America / Arnold M. Eisen.
p.   cm. — (The Helen and Martin Schwartz
lectures in Jewish studies)
Includes bibliographical references and index.
ISBN 0-253-33314-8 (alk. paper)
1. Judaism—20th century.   2. Judaism—United States.
3. Jews—Cultural assimilation—United States.
I. Title.   II. Series.
BM565 .E385   1997
296'.0973'09045—dc21   97-1150

2   3   4   5   02   01   00   99   98

For my friends

The Torah
is a tree of life
to those who take
hold of it.

Proverbs 3:18

CONTENTS

INTRODUCTION

I am by profession a scholar of modern Jews and Judaism, and the materials that I research and teach in the course of my work will inform every page that follows. But this is very much a personal and not an academic book: an attempt by one modern Jew to make sense of the Judaism which he holds, and which holds him. It began a few years back when, approaching my fortieth birthday, I decided to give myself an accounting of where I stood on the matters of most concern to me. Jewish community and tradition figured high on that list, wrapped up in all the rest. The tradition has become so integral a part of who I am, and the American Jewish community so crucial to the life I am trying to lead and pass on to my children, that I cannot but consider matters large and small in terms of the commitments they inspire. In its final form this book has also been shaped by conversations with Jews in synagogues and organizations around the country that I have had the privilege of addressing during the past decade. Those discussions convinced me that the dilemmas I have been wrestling with in my life, as in my scholarship, are widely shared— and gave me the tools as well as the confidence to write about them.

The general character of these dilemmas can be succinctly stated. Jews, like other Americans, have both benefited and suffered from the fraying of traditional loyalties so eloquently described by Robert Bellah and his co-authors in *Habits of the Heart*.[1] We have been trying, in their words, to reconcile "individualism and commitment," to inhabit new roles for which there is no precedent, to balance the needs of families with the increasing demands of careers, to grow old with grace and dignity—and to do all this virtually alone, without the guidance and constraints once provided by integral communities and vibrant religious traditions. I have increasingly felt the strain as my responsibilities have grown with the years. My friends, Jewish and non-Jewish, testify to it as well.

The problem is exacerbated for Jews like me by the very real fear that much that is most precious to us, the deepest source of guidance and wisdom that we know, might soon be lost in this country—because the American Jewish community may well be in the process of dissolution. A recent national survey found that at any given moment only a quarter of American Jews are in any way active in Jewish life, religious or secular, while perhaps another 35 percent are marginally connected to it and fully 40 percent seem totally alienated. More Jews now marry Gentiles than marry other Jews, and the vast majority of those intermarried couples are not raising Jewish children.[2]

Paradoxically—and tragically—all this is occurring at the very same moment when Judaism and the Jewish community are in other respects flowering in this country as never before. Synagogues across America are showing new signs of vitality. Jewish private schools are developing so rapidly they lack for qualified instructors. Jewish bookstores overflow with Jewish books. Jewish Studies programs now prosper at every major university. And—last but far from least—Israel offers cultural and spiritual resources to diaspora Jews about which previous generations could only dream.

There is therefore much reason to hope; for all that the present is, in Jewish terms, not the best of times in many respects, it is certainly not the worst of times either. The problems are unprecedented, but so are the opportunities—a combination which has provoked widespread perplexity. My aim in this book is to provide, if not a guide, at least a program for personal and collective navigation of the terrain in which we find ourselves. The obstacles besetting Judaism and other traditions in America have long been in the making and cannot entirely be overcome. Certainly no quick fix is available. All those currently on the market justifiably arouse suspicion. But—and this must be stressed time and again before Jewish audiences who have grown comfortable with prophecies of their own imminent disappearance—the very challenges we face point the direction needed to work through and around them. We *can* minimize the curses inherent in American Jewish life, and maximize the blessings, if only we can summon the collective will and energy to do so.

The curses, I believe, are in fact the "flip side" of the blessings: the price that Jews began to pay two centuries ago for the incalculable goods of emancipation from the ghetto, and pay still in our day for full participation in every aspect of American society and culture. Modernity, enlightenment, social acceptance, and political liberties—

all of which we dearly treasure, and all of which have reached their greatest fulfillment in America—carry with them the consequence that Jews can choose *whether* as well as *how* to be Jewish. Inevitably many Jews will choose not to engage their ancestral tradition or participate in the Jewish community in any serious fashion, and some will even opt out altogether. There are many options for identity available, many paths to walk, and few people in any time and place ever opt to move against the currents of their society and culture. Other ethnic and religious groups are experiencing similar pressures, with similar results. Even Protestants—a large majority in America—complain with justice about powerful trends in our society and culture which militate against the maintenance of integral communities every bit as much as they challenge faith in God and undermine loyalty to age-old traditions. Everyone must now choose whether or not to undertake commitments which until recently could be taken for granted. The choice for Judaism is all the more difficult because of what it carries with it: nightmares of Auschwitz, the weight of ancestors, the claims of God and conscience, responsibilities here and abroad, and the continuing anxieties (and costs) of apartness.

Yet the very diversity that has weakened every claim has also opened space for Jews, significantly enlarging the scope of Jewish possibility. Jews in America do not stand out as strangers to a religiously or ethnically homogeneous society—the case in many diasporas heretofore, particularly in the modern West. American pluralism has provided Jews and others the freedom to maintain substantial difference without surrendering full participation in the larger society. It has also enabled Jews to acquire the unparalleled resources—financial and cultural—that are needed to actualize the opportunities available. The question is how many Jews can be persuaded to take advantage of what America has put on offer: a synthesis of spirit as rich as any the world has known, a commitment treasured all the more because Jews have chosen it of their own free will.

There is every reason for hope in this regard, I repeat: not merely because the Jewish people has been around for some three millennia, has survived much worse than America, and so might well be able to survive even success, but because something like a quarter of the American Jewish population *has* chosen to place Judaism at or near the center of their lives—to live the tradition and have it live through them. They have done so, I am convinced, because Judaism offers precisely what many in America have lost thanks to the freedoms and choices conferred by modernity: integral *community,* and *meaning* profound enough to live by. Many more Jews would want Judaism for themselves, require it in their marriages, and demand it of their children, if they too were able to find compelling meaning in Jewish tradition and palpable satisfactions in the life of the community which bears its name. We know how to provide these and have the resources with which to do so. That is the ground of the optimism I shall profess in this book concerning the Jewish future despite a very sober vision of the forces besieging the Jewish present, which shall likewise be set forth here. Meaning and community are eternal human needs. They constitute goods that in our time have become particularly scarce. And they are demonstrably available at the address that I shall be describing.

If this analysis is correct, the implications for communal policy are clear. Jewish leaders and institutions should spend a lot less time and money worrying about Jewish "defections" through intermarriage or assimilation (both of which are unalterable givens of life in an open society). They should cease preying on Jewish guilt about the numbers destroyed in the Holocaust and should stop haranguing Jews about obligations to which their audiences cannot relate. Neither is a strategy that can return significant numbers of Jews to either tradition or community. We should rather be working harder at providing experiences of meaning and community, ideally together. That task requires reimagining the tradition in ways that speak profoundly to the minds and hearts of American Jews as they actually are, and redesigning our community to meet the needs they have rather than the needs which rabbis or federations think they *should* have. My aim in this book is to contribute to the discussion underway as how to accomplish that goal. The point is to *fashion a community* that helps Jews live rightly and live well without abandoning full participation in American society, and to *describe a Judaism* that assists their quest for wholeness and transcendence.

It is for such Jews—the committed and the searching—that I write, and for contemporary Americans of whatever tradition who, like my own close non-Jewish friends, share the concerns described here and are walking on parallel paths. I confess at the outset that I cannot provide easy answers to what ails them and ails me—in fact I cannot provide answers of any finality whatsoever. I hope, however, that the personal voice of these reflections—the lack of dogma, the absence of formula—will enable me to speak all the more convincingly to those who, like me, are dissatisfied with most of what is presented to them in the name of institutional "Judaism" but who wish to be at home in their tradition nonetheless.

Before beginning with The Beginning—Genesis—I want to offer three final prefatory words about method. They concern the personal voice, the addressing of contemporary issues, and the focus on Torah that shall feature in each of the book's five chapters.

Use of the first person singular is awkward for me, I confess, and has been foreign to my scholarship. I introduce the "I" in this essay only in order to make the point that every Jew brings different gifts and needs to the study and the living of Torah. The decisions that we make for Judaism are highly individual. They begin in the particular families and communities that have nurtured us. We cannot but bring our personal stories to the larger story that our people has been telling for many centuries. We start where and as we are, take on the tradition as we find it, one by one, commit differently to the same covenant, and so inscribe ourselves in the "never-ending story" of the Jewish people and its Torah. What we add to that larger story, how we take it forward, will of course vary with our distinctive points of origin.

It is absolutely fundamental to the vision of tradition and community to be set forth here that one never signs once and for all on the bottom line of a contract titled Judaism, agreeing to abide by a set of truths entailed therein. Rather one embarks on a lifelong journey—paralleling Abraham's—that necessarily joins creativity with what is given. That is why the first question confronting a Jew is not what he or she *believes*—always a difficult matter, and likely to change somewhat with time. It is *where he or she will stand* in relation to tradition, what the place of the community will be in his or her life, and vice versa. Genesis, comprised primarily of narratives about the ancestors—personal stories, we would call them—is the first book of the Torah. Sinai—confrontation with issues of covenant and faith—comes only in Exodus, the second.

This has always been the case, I believe, but it is now more true than ever, thanks to the immense diversity made possible by modernity, nowhere more so than in America. There is no one "Judaism" and cannot be. Many forms of Jewish commitment are alive and well in these United States—from feminism to Hasidism, from New Age to Orthodox. Unanimity as to destination will forever elude us, and is not a goal for which we should strive. I want to argue as forcefully as I can that the existence of multiple and conflicting Judaisms in America today is cause not for alarm but for celebration, despite the heartbreak of dispute and mutual recrimination that it causes daily. Pluralism inside Judaism, as in America as a whole, makes us stronger.

That is not to say, however, that nothing unites us. One of the principal markers of the Jewish covenant, however defined—and so of every Jewish path continuous with tradition—is that it demands enactment in the world. The Torah does not provide ultimate enlightenment and does not call us away from the world in order to receive it. Jewish commitment rather requires our activity in and on this world, a shadowy mixture of light and dark. Torah is not meant for the angels, the rabbis remarked long ago. Angels neither eat nor drink, and so need not worry about dietary laws. They do not suffer poverty or oppression, need not heal the sick or raise up those who are bowed down. Human beings do. Hence the thematic components of this book, reflecting items on the agenda of our life in the contemporary Jewish world, as imperfect and in need of repair as any human world.

All the themes to be highlighted here loom large in the Torah's five books. We must (as Genesis insists) come to terms with the facts of biography: that we are born to these parents and not others, in this time and place rather than another, and so choose among a limited set of options. We must (a lesson of Exodus) come to terms with history and make our promises to God and one another in its midst. We do not and should not live alone, but rather (as Leviticus makes clear) require community and employ ritual in order to build community as we together sanctify everyday life. Because we are commanded to change the world, we must engage in politics (the foremost theme, to my mind, of the Book of Numbers), and must do so as the ancient Israelites did in the wilderness, looking ever forward to a promise and a certainty we never actually possess. Finally, we must do all this not only for ourselves, but—as partners in creation, responsible stewards of a world we do not own—for future generations. We have no choice as adults but to concern ourselves (as Deuteronomy does) with raising students, teaching children, passing on what we have received. I discuss these five themes as examples of the wider relevance that we all seek in our traditions and can surely find in this one.

That is why, finally, I have organized my book around the Torah's five books. My aim is to contribute to the revitalization of the contemporary American Jewish community—and all that I have learned of the Jewish past tells me that no Jewish community has ever existed except on the basis of a live, engaged relation to the Torah. I mean here both Torah in the narrow sense of the Five Books of Moses and Torah in the broader sense of the commentaries, compendia, philosophies, fictions—and lives!—that have been constructed over the centuries around the five books (and the Bible as a whole) at their center. No less important, I focus on the Torah because it is my personal center, what I most love to teach because—aside from the people that matter most to me—it is what I most love. There is to the best of my knowledge no other communal future available for American Jews in the new century almost upon us than to turn for new direction to Torah, the ground of every Jewish past, and take hold of it anew. I assume as well that engagement with Torah now, as ever, will take place, and prove sustaining, only if it is performed not just out of obligation but out of love.

This essay is driven by such passion and I hope will elicit or strengthen it among my readers, as they turn with me to Torah for challenge, argument, and renewal—and turn with Torah in hand to the task that faces our generation as it has faced every generation before us: the rebuilding of community, the reimagining of tradition, the transformation of oneself and the world.

TAKING HOLD OF TORAH

1

Genesis

TAKING ON TRADITION

For as long as Jews have been reading Torah, they have been wondering why it begins where it does. The question arises in the very first section of the commentary by the greatest of medieval Jewish exegetes, Rashi, who poses it in the name of a sage who had lived nearly a thousand years before. "Rabbi Isaac said: the Torah did not need to begin until 'From this month . . .' [Exodus 12:1], the first mitzvah that Israel was commanded. What point is there in beginning with Bereshit?" Why start a book that is meant to direct Jewish behavior in the world with stories about the trials and tribulations, the loves and losses, of the ancestors? What bearing could Adam and Eve, the flood, and genealogies galore—the stuff of what we today call myth—possibly have on the concrete yeses and noes of everyday life?

Rashi's answer was that the stories of Genesis are there to establish the justice of the Jewish people's claim to the land of Israel. I would like to suggest another answer, a way of reading the Torah's beginning that is particularly germane to the decisions facing contemporary American Jews. It is that the Torah starts where *we* do. It locates each and every one of us in the chain of human actors stretching back to the very beginning, in order to have us reflect on the consequences and responsibilities entailed in being who we are: ourselves and not someone else, the children of our parents and not others, members in a family and fate that claim us as their own. Only after coming to terms with these fundamental givens of identity—a complicated process, as we all know, which in our day normally occupies a good deal of adolescence and occasionally stretches well beyond it, into therapy—are we prepared for the promises that mark adulthood: the commitments to one another, and to God, that will define our lives. The Torah calls those commitments "covenants," and the time and place we make them "Sinai."

According to this view, Genesis is not trying to present science to us in its first chapter, or any ancient version of science, though the progression from energy to matter to organic life in its account of the six days of creation has proven wonderfully suggestive over the ages, and uncannily resembles several of the major stories that our physicists and biologists now tell about cosmic and human origins. Jewish commentators have been content from time immemorial to regard the six days of creation as figures for aeons of unspecified duration and to speculate on God's previous creations of other worlds. Neither Darwin nor Einstein need pose the problems for classically trained Jewish readers that they do for believers in some other traditions. The sacredness of the text for Jews has never depended upon its literal truth—and could not, because Jews have from the beginning argued over what that truth is and how we can be sure of it and how much weight it should have as compared with other sorts of truth: homiletic, allegorical, mystical.

What *does* matter in the creation story is the import it bears for human life, and particularly for the moral choices, individual and collective, in which the Torah hopes to school us. That education is meant to proceed, I believe, via encounters over the course of each individual life with the characters (human and divine) that populate the Torah and loom particularly large in its first book. We go deeper and deeper into their stories as we read them year after year, just as we go deeper into our own lives. We learn better how to love, progress along the paths that we have chosen from among those chosen for us. That learning makes us better readers—and vice versa. More and more we identify with the characters and the situations in which they find themselves, nod knowingly at the parental dilemmas and sibling rivalries, feel the passions that drive people sometimes higher and sometimes lower, reflect upon our own deceptions and self-deceptions, debate the inevitability of what transpires. Not infrequently we find ourselves surprised at developments that have long since become familiar. We are not reading them for the first time, or the tenth.

In this way, we *take on* the tradition, in both senses of the term. We make it ours. And the more it matters to us, the more we wrestle with it. The Torah wants us to enter its world in this way, I think, and so to bring its living word into our world. Genesis comes first in the Torah because we need it, first and always, to help us grow into the promises that we must make, the selves we should become.

For Jews in particular (though to some extent for all Americans, indeed for everyone whose culture has been shaped decisively by modernity) the process of self-commitment has of late become immensely more complicated than ever before. We must decide matters which in earlier generations would have been decided for us, including the matter of whether to *read* the story that begins at the Beginning, let alone to step into it. Most Jews in America now come to the Torah from afar. They were not raised on the story of Abraham leaving his homeland and the house of his father for a land that God would show him. In many cases American Jews must literally leave their own parents' homes in order to encounter Abraham for the first time, and must certainly depart their parents' culture—that of secular America—in order to "cross the river" into observance of the covenant that he first entered.

Even Jews like myself, who did grow up on these stories of the ancestors, and who (if males) likely boiled over in adolescent rage as I did at fathers who would even think of sacrificing their sons on a mountain because they heard a voice that told them to—even such Jews are presented with repeated opportunities to opt out of the Jewish story, usually as early as high school. They have before them as young adults the examples of countless friends who have already done so.

One exaggerates only slightly, I think, in saying that Judaism in contemporary America is a commitment under siege. It is surrounded on all sides by alternatives which at best leave the Torah one of many books on the shelf to be taken down at moments of interest or fancy (as the covenant is one of many possible lives), and at worst reduce the Torah to an ethnoreligious myth of greater or lesser appeal depending on the page. It is great literature, to be sure, but who could seriously entertain the thought of having his or her life altered by a book, however masterful, much less by a story? Let Abraham leave the highest civilization of his day for God knows what. Most American Jews will understandably stick with what they've got, stay where they are, rest content with the culture that is content to have these stories somewhere on the margins of what matters to it.

Three principal challenges confront Jewish identity in contemporary America, I believe, all of them wrapped up in the complexity of relationship to Torah. The first is the loss of integral *community*, a group of individuals bound to each other from birth to the grave by virtue of the fact that all are bound to the same sacred text. The second challenge is the relativizing and marginalizing of this (or any) *tradition* over the past two centuries due to the triumph of scientific and historical consciousness. The third is the emergence of a new sort of *self* with little patience—or apparent need—for the "truths" that Jewish tradition (Torah in the wider sense) had heretofore provided.

I will examine each factor briefly before returning to the question of how all three, working together, have changed the way contemporary Jews approach the decision to take on Jewish tradition. We will then be prepared for two further questions, to me the most urgent on the current Jewish agenda: what it means to live in the framework of these stories, given the freedom we all currently exercise to choose what we read and how we live; and how we can revitalize our tradition to render its stories more compelling, yet remain confident that it is really *this* tradition we are continuing, these stories we are retelling, and not others of our own invention.

Community, Tradition, Self

Until the end of the eighteenth century in western and central Europe, and much later in eastern Europe, North Africa, and the Ottoman Empire, Jews lived by and large in *self-contained worlds* bounded by walls which, whether figurative or actual, were extremely difficult to scale. It hadn't always been that way. In Palestine, or Persia, or Moslem Spain in the "Golden Age" or late Renaissance Italy, Jews were far more a part of the host society, their status far less "disprivileged" (a favorite term of the sociologist Max Weber). But in the eighteenth century, in Europe, the walls were definitely up—and sometimes they were as real as could be, locked at night from the outside. Jewish life therefore had a uniformity and predictability hard for twentieth-century Americans to imagine.

Genesis: Taking on Tradition

A boy like me would have been circumcised at birth and educated exclusively on Jewish texts in a Jewish school. He would eat and play and talk almost exclusively with other Jews. The life stretching out before him would be patterned on models centuries old. He would probably marry at a young age (a Jewish girl, of course, selected by his father) and spend his life on study (if he demonstrated the aptitude) or on business, lofty or low, if he did not. For girls, life was still more circumscribed—limited, often enough, to the four walls within the home. Jews who sued other Jews in court would be judged by a Jewish judge according to Jewish law, just as Jews generally paid taxes not to a Gentile state or king but to a Jewish communal organization that collected the money and then passed it on. In this as in most other matters the community enjoyed the authority and the power to compel the strict obedience of its members.

Doubt and disbelief were present to some extent, we can assume, for they always are, but one kept them to oneself, pretty much. A skeptic could always sit in the back of the synagogue and read commentaries, or talk with friends outside. Things like dietary laws were far more important. Likely as not, the average Jew never ate in a Gentile's home or (unless business or persecution required it) traveled more than a few miles from the place of his or her birth.

This meant that the wider world—of which Jews were aware to varying degrees—remained to a remarkable extent a homogeneous fiction of the Jewish people's collective imagination. Even at times of exceptional openness by the Gentile society, and corresponding acculturation by the Jews, that world was perceived as fraught with dangers, and Jews had very little to do with it. On one side, inside, there were the Children of Israel, God's "saving remnant," His "chosen people," and on the other the undifferentiated "nations of the world" who, as the psalmist said, "knew not the Lord." The wall of separation dividing Jews from Gentiles made Jewish chosenness a commonsense and tangible notion, while chosenness in turn explained why Jews always had been "a people dwelling apart" and would always remain such until the coming of the messiah. God, and the history God directed, had conspired to make them so.

Toward the close of the eighteenth century, however, the situation I've just described began to change dramatically.[1] Emancipation, the grant or promise of civil and political rights to Jews, meant that they had to find a place as individuals in new economic and political orders. Opportunities beyond measure presented themselves. Hope of social acceptance by the Gentiles stirred and was nourished by famous friendships such as that between the Jewish philosopher Moses Mendelssohn and the German playwright Gotthold Lessing. Access to information and imaginings beyond anything that Jews in the ghetto could have conceived turned their pictures of the world upside down. In return they had only to shed much of their distinctiveness and dismantle the integral community (already in some disarray for political and economic reasons) that had long held them in its warm but often stifling embrace. It seemed a fair trade. Read the autobiography of Solomon Maimon, who made the liberating journey from a shtetl in Poland to the salons of Berlin, and you get a sense of the excitement many must have felt at the opening of the long-locked gate to the outside, the seemingly endless vistas of possibility.[2] I know what I myself felt, turning the latch easily on the door which led me far from my childhood neighborhood in Philadelphia. The joy two hundred years ago must have been multiplied at least two hundredfold.

This is not the place for a nuanced account of modern Jewish history. Suffice it to say that the situation I have described gave rise to the variety of Jewish options known to us today, from assimilation at one extreme to Zionism and separatist Orthodoxy on the other, with numerous strategies of compromise and adjustment in between. Voluntarist communities took shape in the West. Antisemitism was suffered and combatted. New definitions of Judaism emerged to suit the new social, political, and economic orders in which Jews found themselves. In eastern Europe religious reform did not take hold, for political acceptance by Gentiles was not forthcoming or even promised. Jews did not adopt someone else's national identity but retained their own, in secular as well as religious forms, and could hope to attain freedom en masse only by taking it with them to the Jewish state sought and eventually established by Zionism.

The key point for us to remember is that everywhere outside that state—including America, where Jewish life and faith have most thrived in the modern diaspora—the loss of integral Jewish community has meant that Jewish commitment is a matter of choice. That is nowhere more true than in contemporary America, where the freedom to participate fully in the life of the larger society is in every respect greater than it has ever been before, indeed is nearly absolute.

Genesis: Taking on Tradition

We are living, moreover, in what is very likely the most mobile society that has ever existed on the face of the earth, or exists today (I myself have moved three times as an adult, and that is not atypical), these moves aided and urged by a culture that is profoundly individualist. It is no wonder that the Jewish community in this situation has to argue for every single Jewish soul, compete for every pledge of allegiance against an ever-increasing wealth of beckoning possibilities, and must do so not once in a person's life but repeatedly, year in and year out, because each of us repeatedly decides not only where to live but with whom and how. America is a difficult environment in which to maintain communities of any sort, let alone communities of a tiny minority (slightly over 2 percent of the population at last count) such as the Jews.

Let me stress, as I did earlier, that the developments just surveyed have not been entirely negative. Far from it. Like most contemporary American Jews, I treasure both sides of my hyphenated identity, not only one. America is not a world outside my self but moves as much inside me as I move freely on its streets and inside its institutions. The person I am, indeed the Jew I am, could never have existed were it not for the breaking down of barriers that once kept Jews apart and only thus kept their community together. Modernity has bestowed not only material but spiritual goods of the highest order. I write as a card-carrying member of modern liberal culture, an American Jew who would not trade life in American society for any that has ever existed. I don't see how any Jew in his or her right mind could long for a return to the conditions of the Middle Ages. We should recognize, too, that commitments made voluntarily often come with a kind of energy and vitality that can never be evoked by communities to which one belongs whether one likes it or not. But having said all that, I think we also need to be clear about what has been lost. Our freedom to choose Judaism, or not choose it, has exacted a terrible cost. The deracinated Judaism that I found on view as a child in my synagogue remains the only sort of Judaism that millions of American Jews, scattered in their many cities and suburbs, ever know. It constitutes the most visible example of the effects wrought by modernity's disintegration of traditional community.

The second obstacle standing in the way of contemporary Jewish commitment is, if anything, more difficult to overcome: the emergence and eventual triumph in Western culture of *scientific and historical consciousness*. In college I somehow got the wrong-headed notion that science had simply challenged faith to a duel at some point in the nineteenth century, and won; in lieu of finishing religion off with a single blow, the victor had chosen rather to run the loser out of town. William Jennings Bryan, as it were, was routed from civilization's center by Clarence Darrow in the Scopes Trial, and allowed to live and prosper afterward only so long as he stayed somewhere out on the frontier. But this view of things is nonsense. Does the triumph of science mean, asked Weber,

> that we, today, for instance, everyone sitting in this hall, have a greater knowledge of the conditions of life under which we exist than has an American Indian or a Hottentot? Hardly. Unless he is a physicist, one who rides on the streetcar has no idea how the car happened to get into motion. And he does not need to know. He is satisfied that he may "count" on the behavior of the streetcar, and he orients his conduct according to this expectation. . . .[3]

That sounds more like it to me than the Dodge City duel. I myself have no idea how anything works (not a TV, not even a light bulb). I know only that to get things to work I need not invoke God's assistance, and that people who do claim to understand how things work, the scientists and masters of technology, rarely if ever mention God in their reports. God has simply become irrelevant to the functioning and explanation of daily life, public and private. God resides completely outside the system. No Stanford scientist who invoked God in accounting for any event in nature could possibly get tenure.

That, and not refutation of faith, is the effect of science upon Jewish tradition. It has rendered it a marginal anachronism. Prayer has lost its context in real world activity and religion its arena. "We have an old Father—praised be His name, who has never changed and never will change," wrote one eighteenth-century rabbi, perplexed at the transformation all around him and resolved to oppose it at all costs. So it has seemed to many Jews and Christians in the past two centuries, I think, and many have chosen to leave their fathers' (and mothers') homes, literal and figurative, as a result. This has in turn left our old God without much to do on earth, or even a place to pass the time except for increasingly vacant synagogues and churches, where He/She rests, studies, and—so one Jewish tradition goes—arranges marriages.

Judaism is not merely faith, as I have already argued more than once. Tradition encompasses far more than belief. Some of the finest modern Jewish thinkers—most notably Ahad Ha'am and Mordecai Kaplan—have labored to separate the two, the better to save Judaism from the wreck of premodern belief in God. I hope to build on their efforts here. But it remains true that contemporary Judaism of whatever sort is the heir to a profoundly religious civilization, and that the meaning of identifying with that civilization in America today—walking to its rhythms, thinking in its terms—hinges on the ability at the very least to take the religion that nurtured it seriously. If God is an adolescent fantasy, traditional rituals the mere enactment of obsessive-compulsive neuroses, religion rightly shunted to the side of modern adult existence, then Judaism, however defined, can hardly be an attractive option.

The effect of historical consciousness on traditional faith and loyalties has, if anything, been still more dramatic. Weber caricatured rather than captured the viewpoint that modern sensibility supplanted, I believe, by referring to the authority of tradition as "the eternal yesterday," "the unimaginably ancient recognition and habitual orientation to conform."[4] As if people before our enlightened age never thought for themselves, never calculated, and always obeyed simply because they believed things had always been done that way and always would be. Weber knew better than that. So did countless modern thinkers who elegized and sentimentalized the "age of faith," the better to ensure that no self-respecting modern would ever be tempted to opt for faith.

Nevertheless, Weber had a point: a Jew could pretty much take his or her world for granted, before it crumbled with Emancipation. Gentile challengers were kept outside the gates and marked pejoratively as outsiders. One could change and adapt in response to those challenges as Jews had for centuries, generally by pretending not to change. Inside the walls all discussion was conducted, all arguments fought out, according to certain basic assumptions that went back, in the last resort, to the most axiomatic authority of all—God's Torah.

Modern historical consciousness, which began to take hold in the late eighteenth century, meant that appeals to Torah no longer settled any argument, for God had not written the text, and Moses probably had not either. Any custom for which someone claimed the authority of "Torah from Sinai" could be shown to be the product of a far more recent and historically ascertainable yesterday. Christianity underwent the same challenge once nineteenth-century thinkers undertook the "quest for the historical Jesus," forcing believers to realize how unavailing that quest would be: how much "gospel truth" was only one version of events that had to compete against other versions and the facts for a Christian's allegiance. Every religious "truth" in our day represents only a claim, every rule an institution brought into being by some person or persons who, like you and me, were not without personal interest in the outcome. The people behind the rules had calculated loss and gain, and so should we in deciding whether or not to observe them. That is all the more true when a decision to respect the authority of tradition involves, as it does for Jews, setting oneself apart from the mainstream of one's society and culture.

Again, this development is both good and bad for the Jews and Judaism. We cannot reverse it in any case, and on balance should not want to. I value modernity for its culture, not only for the longer and better life its technology has afforded me. I am profoundly indebted to Kant and Nietzsche, George Eliot and Dostoevsky, and to countless other modern thinkers. The Jew I am could not have existed without Martin Buber and Franz Rosenzweig and dozens of other Jewish souls called forth by those same modern greats. Much that is most precious to me in contemporary Judaism—the changes brought about by feminism being only the most recent example—could not have come to pass without the fracturing of Jewish tradition by history and science.

But I want us to recognize, with the best of the modern greats, that much has been lost in all this gain—and it has not been the loss depicted by the modern canon, which too often pictures a past so idyllic or benighted—and either way so utterly distant—that we could not reasonably wish to carry it forward. We need not be unduly romantic, elegizing a past that never was, or denigrate the present in facile caricature, to face up to the good that once existed and is no longer. Judaism is both richer and poorer for this trade. We are all both richer and poorer for it.

∽❀∾

Enter player number three in the story I summarize here: *a new sort of "rational" self* large enough, as Kant put it in his famous essay, "What Is Enlightenment?", to shake off the "tutelage" of centuries and think for itself, as an adult.[5] Scholars have tried for several generations to describe the difference between the notions that we have today concerning what it means to be a person, and what people thought in eastern or central Europe as recently as a hundred years ago. It is hard to do. Lionel Trilling's study *Sincerity and Authenticity,* or Peter Berger's *The Heretical Imperative,* as fine as any attempts I know to get at what is distinctive in our awareness, strike me when all is said and done as suggestive at best rather than conclusive.[6]

But we can assume with Trilling and Berger, I think, that a person with a life expectancy of forty, no indoor plumbing, few books to open, and fewer possibilities—that such a person thought of himself or herself very differently than we do on the eve of the twenty-first century. We generally choose careers (and now spouses) more than once in life, as we choose elected officials every year or two and consumer goods every day. These actions are mutually reinforcing. We also jet from here to there at the drop of a credit card, are alive to the worlds opened up by microscope and telescope, think through the eyes of Freud and Darwin. Even the least educated among us enact the collective new-found freedom from necessity as often as they switch channels on the TV or—perhaps most crucial of all—use birth control. Therefore, while it is hard to know exactly how we differ from our ancestors—and let us not forget for a moment that "they" too were a diverse group—there seems little doubt that we do differ, and substantially so.

Our relation to God and community and history cannot but differ also. Invocations of authority, for all we understand their necessity, affront our dignity. Communal pressure of any sort occasions ambivalence and resentment. History cannot obligate us, nor can anything else that we have not (in our minds) chosen—family, for example. I speak for myself here first of all. God, finally, seems frustratingly but not unpleasantly distant, having left us ample room for maneuver. We have made sure of that. How could we function with a watchful eye up close?

I know I generalize far beyond the evidence. "Modernity" covers a lot of ground, and several billion souls. I too read the survey data which remind us that Americans still describe themselves as an extraordinarily religious people. They go to church, albeit infrequently, and pray with some regularity. Yet that same survey data, not to mention our literature and in fact all our arts, elite and popular, reveal a new, proud, individualist consciousness—largely independent of religious determination—that our ancestors would not have recognized in the mirror. Daniel Yankelovich's 1978 survey of American values pointed to

> an ethic built around the concept of duty to oneself, in glaring contrast to the traditional ethic of obligation to others. [People] want freedom to express impulses and desires that [they] have been accustomed to suppress. Sexual desires are the most obvious . . . but other forms of freedom to do what I want to do are almost as prominent: freedom to enjoy life now rather than in some distant future; freedom to elevate one's own desire to the rank of entitlements; freedom to give one's own ego more room in which to maneuver; freedom to pull up stakes and move on without having to pick up the pieces.[7]

Robert Bellah and his co-authors painted a similar picture in the eighties in *Habits of the Heart*. There is nothing to indicate that the nineties are any different.

Our modern individualism does not discredit us, necessarily, unless we invoke it in narcissistic celebration of self or avoidance of responsibilities toward others. It is simply who we are, and at times it even powers some of what is noblest in us; for example, the pursuit of civil and human rights. I wish once more only to point out the problems that the view of self we carry with us, and through which we see all things, has created for the Jewish relation to community and tradition. Jews, whether they are personally religious or secular, find themselves inundated with demands from one communal organization after another for support, usually in the name of Jewish obligation or Jewish destiny. "You belong to us," the community declares. "Consider the Holocaust. Reflect upon the State of Israel. Your desire for utter autonomy, for freedom from binding ties to the Jewish people, runs counter to your weighty history and distinctive fate." Many Jews reject such calls to collective identity—precisely in the name of individual freedom.

The very same cultural forces also pose a barrier to their relation with Jewish tradition. American Jews, whether religious or secular, are heirs to ancestors who took God with ultimate seriousness. In most cases the memory of pious parents or grandparents is still vivid, arousing complex sentiments of attraction, ambivalence, and guilt. The very name Israel, with which almost all Jews nowadays identify proudly, means (as we shall see in a moment) "God-wrestler," a name bestowed upon Jacob as a result of his fateful struggle with God's angel.

Contrast this inherited status with Nietzsche's marvelous modernist declaration, made through his alter ego, Zarathustra: "If there were gods, how could I endure not to be a god! Hence there are no gods." What could one create if gods existed? The idea that we are subject to forces beyond our control seems repugnant but true to many contemporary Americans. The idea that we are short-lived servants of an eternal God who, like that God's designs, will forever remain beyond our comprehension seems absolutely intolerable—and, given much else in minds furnished by modern culture, ridiculous. Such a God seems both too good to be true, after Freud's suspicion of all wish-fulfillment, and too authoritative to be countenanced, now that modernity has set us all on the task of mastering our world, indeed the universe. Even faithful modern selves have a difficult time taking the claim of God's presence in the world seriously.

Small wonder that the religion presented to Jews in their synagogues seems "irrelevant, oppressive, dull, insipid" and that the pews are generally empty. The acrobatics demanded by faith are not easy to perform. The reasons for performing them are not often compelling.

And so the Jewish story, which until a few decades ago seemed a "never-ending story" to almost all who participated in it, does have an end for an increasing number of American Jews. They decide, if only through indecision, to opt out or to remain connected only in the most tenuous of ways. Social forces, if left to act without concerted resistance, may soon put an end to every sort of collective American Jewish story except Orthodox versions which, understanding what they are up against, insist on a degree of social and cultural apartness that the vast majority of American Jewish selves will not countenance.

What then can one do? The answer, I think, is given with the specifics of the problem.

The decline of integral community, particularly in mobile, individualist America, has left a hunger for connection among many Jews that a revitalized Jewish community would be uniquely capable of assuaging.

Judaism, as rich and profound a tradition as human beings have ever created, can be reimagined so as to reach American Jews with meaning unavailable elsewhere in American society and culture.

Finally, selves in search of depth and guidance, men and women who want the weight of meaning and dignity that Judaism calls *kavod*, will if they experience that substance return for more. My confidence that this could be the case is based on the fact that it *already is* the case for hundreds of thousands of American Jews, including me, who take advantage daily of opportunities which can be made available to millions more.

The query raised whenever I or others advance this claim is: yes, but at what price?—the concern not being money so much as freedom. Community conjures up the nightmare of the ghetto and the provincialism of the shtetl. Tradition, when it is distinguished from mere nostalgia, provokes anxiety about the sort of authority which brooks no disobedience or creativity. And the vision of a substantively Jewish self seems to fly in the face of autonomy: to a modern self perhaps the most precious gift of all. The concerns are understandable. I do not share them, I think, not merely out of principle, but because of personal experience.

That is the reason for the short autobiographical excursus which follows. I want to present several stages of the road that I myself have traveled, and particularly the upbringing which has made me at once an American through and through, at home in this country, proud to call it my own, and a Jew with a hunger for varieties of Jewish community and commitment far more substantive than those now generally available. One message I hope to underline through the telling of these elements of my personal story is that we all inevitably bring our backgrounds and their baggage with us to the tradition and the community—and are meant to do so, according to the intentions of the tradition itself. Who we are and have been is not incidental but critical to the ways that we as individuals (and communities composed of individuals) will carry the tradition forward—"take it on" in the two senses that I have been describing. This is in fact the principal gift we bring to the tradition and the community, a source of enrichment of which neither should be deprived. I describe my journey, too, because "where I am coming from," as sixties language would have it, goes a long way toward explaining my sense of where I believe we should be going.

The rabbis conveyed a similar message in an ethical compendium called Pirke Avot some two millennia ago. "Know where you have come from, where you are going, and before Whom you must someday render judgment." I will try to follow the first part of that advice here, albeit briefly—the better to turn, in this and subsequent chapters, to a vision of the road ahead and to a statement of the standard by which I believe our efforts at revitalizing commitment and community should be evaluated.

Stages on My Way

Like many American Jews, I have been nourished on a hyphenated vision of American Jewish wholeness for as long as I can remember. My neighborhood, overwhelmingly Jewish when I first encountered it, changed while I was still a child to a mixture of Jewish, Ukrainian, Vietnamese, and black. The differences were sometimes of great importance, and sometimes of none. But I learned during trips around Philadelphia with my parents that each neighborhood, each store, each intersection on Roosevelt Boulevard contained a secret message about identity. Logan, despite the changes taking place, was still an area where many Jews lived. It was therefore doubly home. Five blocks away, across the Boulevard, the ethnic mix became heavily black, and Fifth Street, closer still, was the Germans' territory. (I always had a bad feeling about them and their Schwarzwald Inn, though I couldn't say why). Further north were nondescript Gentiles with their gray stone row houses and Sears Roebuck, a "goyish store" in which we never shopped. Then, when you got past Oxford Circle and the turnoff for the Tacony-Palmyra Bridge, you were back "home" again, for shopping in the Northeast at Korvettes.

There were moral distinctions attached to the geographical borders, I knew, though again I couldn't have said exactly what they were. Jews were more than merely different, even if not exactly better. They had expectations to live up to. I would grow into them.

However, my world in childhood, as afterward, was not entirely bounded by the primal distinction between Jew and Gentile. I knew early on that I belonged to two different worlds at once, and to both of them fully, even while aware that firm separations had to be made between them. The differences had to be respected. In fact it was the very differences between the worlds that somehow guaranteed my belonging to both of them. I could feel at home to a degree in all of

Philadelphia because one of the pieces of its ethnic mosaic was so clearly marked as mine. In elementary school I said the Pledge of Allegiance and the hymn for Flag Day with deep feeling. The flag belonged to me as much as to anyone. I put out five in a little holder on every holiday. The cobblestones around Independence Hall were part of my home turf. I liked the Christmas carols we sang in school, except for the "Christ the Lord" part at the end of "O Come All Ye Faithful," when I looked around nervously to see if the other Jewish kids were saying the words, or if the Gentile kids were noticing I wasn't. That too was a not unwelcome boundary marker, though it caused me some anxiety. It reinforced my pride in who I was and pointed to the fact that I could sing the rest of the song, even being who I was, without any hesitation.

At Central High (composed in nearly equal portions, it seemed, of Jews, Italians, and blacks, with a smattering of white Protestants and Catholics) I learned to love the Western canon served up by Mr. Mulloy—Plato and Aristotle, Coleridge and Eliot—and came to regard it as my inheritance, not someone else's. For two summers I worked as a volunteer in the Mayor's Office for Information and Complaints at City Hall, and found myself quite at home there too among the many sorts of people who walked through the door. The summer after senior year I worked in the office of the superintendent of schools. He was a maverick, a newcomer to the city, constantly under fire for his innovations. I was the native there, at seventeen. I knew every subway stop in Philadelphia by heart.

If anything, it was my relation to Judaism that was complicated at that point, not my sense of belonging to America. I believe that remains the case for the vast majority of American Jews. As a child, I had derived uncommon enjoyment from Hebrew school and even looked forward to synagogue, where one could run the vacant corridors with abandon. One of the ushers would give me candies, and I loved him for it. But what had pleased the child distressed the teenager immensely. Soon after Bar Mitzvah a huge divide opened up between the riches of Jewish content that I tasted three times weekly in Gratz College's Hebrew high school, ironies and ideas as deep as the best served up at Central, and the utter poverty of synagogue life that I suffered through each Saturday morning. At Gratz we were not only reading the Torah in the original, with medieval Hebrew commentaries, but studying the approaches of modern scholars who ascribed its authorship to "J, E, P and D" rather than to Moses or

God. One Talmud teacher took the old-fashioned approach, memorization page by page, but another—as thoroughgoing a rationalist as I have ever known—taught us to sift through rabbinic sources critically and appreciate them all the more for the effort. Synagogue, on the other hand, meant boring sermons, rote performances, people strutting about with great self-importance and making other people's lives quite miserable. It seemed far from anything serious or worthy. The showy materialism and consumerism of the communal life of American Jewry that I read about in the pages of the *Philadelphia Jewish Exponent* aroused alienation and disgust. Jews and Judaism had suffered great and irreparable loss. Something, somewhere, had gone terribly wrong.

I remember wondering and even asking publicly one Friday night when, after services, the tea and cakes were enlivened by brief messages from Our Youth, why all of us American Jews weren't simply moving to Israel. We had prayed for the return to Palestine for two millennia, hadn't we? It was home, wasn't it? The Israelis seemed alive, vital, powerful in a way we decidedly were not. So, *nu*, why were we in Philadelphia? The audience indulged me. How wonderful that I felt that way! The only thing that kept me in synagogue with them, after a certain point, was the Bible in the pew. The pablum from the pulpit could not touch it, thank God. The more I advanced in high school, the more I came to appreciate the text's bold unpredictability. The Torah was sublime, I decided, and American Judaism was a parody. But how had it happened?

My parents, as always, preached tolerance. But one day, a young assistant rabbi to whom I will forever be grateful took a few of us teenagers aside and liberated us from services and much else by introducing us to Martin Buber and Abraham Heschel. I will never forget—the moment seems mythic in its importance to me—opening Heschel's book *God in Search of Man* to find this first paragraph:

> It is customary to blame secular science and anti-religious philosophy for the eclipse of religion in modern society. It would be more honest to blame religion for its own defeats. Religion declined not because it was refuted, but because it became irrelevant, dull, oppressive, insipid.[8]

"My God!" I exclaimed (aloud, according to memory). "He's been to my shul!" Heschel knew! I noted excitedly that he had not excluded Judaism from the category of religion gone stale. My anger was legitimate. I was not supposed to be tolerant of what I saw all around me! Heschel became still more a hero when, in succeeding years, I watched him march beside Martin Luther King, Jr., serve as co-chair of an organization of clergy opposed to the Vietnam War, and criticize Judaism's current estate without mincing words. His very critique of America in the name of Jewish tradition demonstrated the Jews' full at-homeness in this country. It also showed, of course, that Judaism could actually matter, was really connected to what I most cared about, that for me too it could live.

In college the sense of at-homeness became still more complete. Intellect had the same sort of welcoming universality that I had experienced as a child at the piano. Calculus and sociology, like the harmonies of Bach and Debussy, were wide open to me as to every human being, and I entered into them happily. I also spent a lot of time working on modern Protestant theology, and it—like history and sociology—assisted in understanding the plight of modern Jews, myself of course included. What is more, I began university in 1969— which meant that I also felt at one with an entire student generation. "Hundreds on the College Green, that's it," I exulted at the time, "with wine and guitar roses plucked among a field of frisbees. Grateful Dead parties where we danced until our legs took over and talked until silence carried conversation." So while Jews might have been excluded from the university once upon a time, or segregated in separate fraternities, that was not my sense of the place. My minority had a place within the whole. Though my Jewish observance had lapsed—I stopped going to synagogue except for High Holiday services at home, and stopped observing dietary laws—my Jewish identity stood confirmed, and so—despite the demonstrations against the war—did my attachment to my country. When I left Penn for graduate work at Oxford I did not know what lay ahead, but I did know, and with some certainty, what I was leaving: home.

England—the third and last stage on my way that is relevant here—changed all that, and changed me forever. There was first of all the patent unreality of Oxford, striking from the very first moment that I encountered my college. A six-hundred-year-old quadrangle, spartan but elegant, its chapel lined with stunning stained-glass windows and its alter decked with dozens of statues. A second quad, Georgian this time, the yellow sandstone set off by charming window-boxes and a magnificent wrought-iron gate. The college's famous garden, tended to grow in studied disorder by a hulking man with hair to the shoulders known to the students as Heathcliff. The motto bequeathed by the Founder, William of Wykeham—"Manners makyth man"—found at the bottom of every bowl of Weetabix in the morning and under every plate of Ploughman's Lunch. Servants who seemed to have been there forever (and whose families had in some cases actually worked at New College for generations), and who insisted on calling me "sir." And around it all, the mossy stones of the thousand-year-old city wall, all that remained in that part of town from the fire that raged against and finally stopped the scourge of the Bubonic Plague. What could a twenty-two-year-old American do with this antiquity but gape a bit and then try to act as if he were perfectly at home?

But Oxford, it seemed, had no intention of letting me get away with the pose. My American accent gave me away as an outsider every time I opened my mouth. And even if I had managed to deceive others by keeping silent or affecting the manner of the BBC (we all practiced, for the fun of it), there was no way I could deceive myself about the true state of affairs. I was not just an American kid from Philadelphia, at play in Masterpiece Theater as he studied Weber and the Puritans late into the night. I was an American *Jewish* kid, and except for the dry goods merchant in the Market who invited a few of us to break-fast with his family after services on Yom Kippur, nothing and no one who belonged to Oxford seemed to me to be Jewish, even remotely.

I had moved for the very first time into someone else's world, and it seemed the very capital of Gentile-dom. "Manners makyth man." Indeed. Quite so. The streets I walked, the college I inhabited, the medieval villages through which I biked, had for centuries been forbidden territory to Jews. I was trespassing. The sensation excited me, even as I kept one ear cocked for the relevant authority who would be fetched to throw me out. Just look where the Jewish boy had wandered.

Jewish faculty at Oxford expressed that otherness brilliantly in annual meetings of the Cholent Society, a gathering modeled on

venerable Oxford clubs but named for the simmering stew tradition-
ally eaten by Jews on the Sabbath. At New College several Jewish
students (aided and abetted by Gentile co-conspirators) parodied
both the Oxford clubs and the Cholent group by forming a society of
their own named after one Joshua Lipschitz—"soldier, statesman and
scholar; hero of the battle of Kabul"—a character invented out of
whole cloth. Each February we held a dinner in his honor, cooked to
perfection by the college chef and served by college waiters on college
pewter and china, and accompanied by vintage wines and port from
the college cellar. It was wonderful to play in someone else's world, at
once admiring and poking fun. Never had I felt so Jewish, or so
American. I could "cross and recross the strips of moon-blanch'd
green" that Matthew Arnold's shepherd walked, his poem open in my
hand, "and again renew the quest," though I knew the particular
quest that he described would never be mine.[9] No matter. It was
enough to revel for awhile in my surprising presence in his big wide
Gentile world.

Except, of course, when that world turned threatening—as it did
when the Yom Kippur war broke out. At the break-fast after services
we learned that Israel was in dire straits. The Jews who cared and the
Israelis who had no choice but to care found each other quickly. For
we were alone. BBC practiced its famous even-handedness with one
report from Cairo each evening, one from Amman, one from Da-
mascus, and one from Tel Aviv. *The Times* and *The Guardian* were
both hostile to Israel. Most students seemed indifferent. And English
Jews were quiet. A friend and I made the rounds at the fair of student
organizations and came upon the table of the Jewish Society—
finding, to our amazement, no mention of events in the Middle East.
"We're not an Israel Society, we're a Jewish Society," they explained.

When a leading Jew was shot by a terrorist who, back in the
Middle East, claimed responsibility, I asked a rabbi why British Jews
had not demanded that the government insist upon his extradition.
He told me that his board had discouraged public protest and instead
had asked the archbishop of Canterbury to intervene behind the
scenes. The lessons registered, and in time became a book: I was in
galut, exile, a place where Jews had to keep their heads down. I made
a vow—feeling guilty for reasons I could not fathom about not being
in Israel to join the battle—that as soon as I finished my studies I
would spend a considerable time in Jerusalem, to figure out my
relation to the Jewish homecoming.

Genesis: Taking on Tradition

I cannot speak with authority about English Jewry then or now, and am only indirectly familiar with the community's boldness, more evident in recent years, at standing up for Jewish rights and confronting the issues common to all Jews in the modern West. But I left Oxford for Israel in 1975 armed with two convictions that guide me still. First, that America is a special place. While by no means exempt from the ground rules of modernity, neither immune from assimilation nor untouched by anti-Semitism, America presents Jews with opportunities unprecedented in either modern or premodern history. Jews have achieved a degree of at-homeness in this country that is unparalleled, and we need not sacrifice self-assertion or self-respect in order to maintain it.

The second lesson that I carried away with me was that Jewish tradition has within it the intellectual and spiritual resources to overcome the challenges posed by modernity and modernism (the subject of much of my work at Oxford, and still more of my conversation). The familiar dichotomy of tradition or modernity was a false choice. Max Weber was wrong in assuming that religious commitment demanded intellectual sacrifice. Nor did the glib dismissals of a poem like Wallace Stevens's "Sunday Morning" constitute the last word on the subject of tradition. As the century nears its end, postmodern critics (allied to this extent with feminist theorists) have punctured the pretensions of universality and objectivity in the name of which Judaism was for so long marginalized and critiqued. This has freed many Jews to see, as I did at Oxford, that their tradition contains resources equal to any available elsewhere. The very open-endedness of our stories, the fact that the Torah tells stories rather than "doing philosophy"—both of which were once cause for scorn in the academy—are now a source of celebration by theorists and Jews alike.

This is a wonderful moment for the teaching and living of a tradition. There seems less need nowadays to engage in the apologetic exercise of "objectively" demonstrating the value of reading and re-reading Torah. It is generally enough to say: "This is our community's 'grand narrative,' the foundation of all that we as a people are and do. It has for many generations proven a source of great personal and collective meaning. Why not join the people constituted by the fact that we tell this story and not another, respond to the rituals and symbols that it establishes, grow deeper in its embrace, take up its challenge to transform the world?" If personal experience of the text resonates with "inner power," as it has in recent years for many Jews exposed to adult encounter with Torah for the first time, they will come back for more.

Even those of us who grew up with Torah from childhood are not immune from powerful adult encounters with it. During services on Shavuot, as I prepared to leave Oxford for study in Jerusalem, I was given the honor of raising the Torah scroll, and sat holding it on my lap while it was wrapped and the portion from the Prophets was read aloud. Without warning, I was overcome by the meaning of the verse from Proverbs (3:18) which I knew would be sung in a moment by the congregation as the Torah was returned to the ark. "It is a tree of life to all who hold fast to it." At that moment I knew in a way I had not previously that for me this was and always would be true.

In the years since, in frameworks for learning provided by synagogues, Federations, and organizations such as CLAL, Hadassah, the American Jewish Committee, or the Wexner Heritage Foundation, I have watched many other Jews, whether novices or veterans in the ways of Torah, experience the Torah's power for themselves. There is every reason to believe that countless American Jews would react in similar fashion, if only they were given the opportunity to take hold of it and to inscribe their personal stories, one by one, in the pages of Judaism's book of life.

The Family Romance

The Torah seems to have been designed for precisely this endeavor. It does not simply sit there, as it were, waiting to be read. Rather it reaches out to grab us. All one needs to do is open the book, and we are drawn into the stories of Genesis, at times despite ourselves. Modernity, Martin Buber wrote in 1929, means that one no longer has "access to a sure and solid faith," and knows that such faith cannot "be made accessible." But even so, we can open ourselves to the Torah in the way that we listen, really listen, to good friends, and having done so we will often find ourselves addressed. Bracket for a time the moral and theological problems you may have with "revelation," Buber urged—not forever, but long enough to hear what the Torah has to say. Leave nothing behind in the encounter: not intellect or learning or experience, and certainly not emotion. Not always, but often enough, the text will touch you, challenge you, teach you. It might even command you, demanding—and receiving—what Buber liked to call presence.[10] I report his teaching because I took Buber's advice at several key points in my teenage years and early twenties, and the method worked for me. I found the results as he described them. The Torah was speaking to me with "inner power," generally telling me more than I expected, or wanted, to hear.

In part, I think, the Torah has this effect because it directly addresses the existential situation of adult human beings, and does so without dogma or puffery. The book resolutely eschews simple truths, has no respect for pieties, avoids sentimentality like the plague. It can hardly be coincidental that the correct translation of the Torah's very first words, on which so much else depends, will forever remain in doubt. Does the text really begin "in the beginning," with God's creation of heaven and earth *ex nihilo,* from nothing? Or does it begin at the moment of God's "beginning to create heaven and earth," in which case it describes the divine ordering of matter already given? Rashi prefers the latter reading. So does the recent translation by the Jewish Publication Society. I do too, because of the multiple possibilities of interpretation it makes available. But regardless of which reading one adopts, one recognizes that the ambiguity at the outset of Genesis (and inherent, in its view, in the world) foreshadows (and perhaps accounts for) the darkness over which we will hover at all other key points in the text.

God remains particularly mysterious, elusive, beyond human grasp or comprehension even when present in our midst. But that is true of most of the questions to which we would dearly like answers—the nature of being, the reason for evil, the meaning of death, all of which remain enshrouded in the myth through which the Torah raises them. Few answers are provided. Indeed the covenant with Noah that follows the flood recognizes that murder and mayhem will continue, as much a part of existence as day and night, seedtime and harvest—knowledge and ignorance. The ancestors are markedly flawed. Be prepared for spiritual journeys, the text seems to advise us. Important things happen to those who cross rivers to possibility. Home is generally to be discovered only in the leaving of it.

To Jews, these lessons speak with special urgency. For one thing, the stories are redolent with the pains and growth of wandering.[11] Adam and Eve are banished from the garden, locked in struggle with the earth, alienated from one another, estranged from God. Cain's punishment is greater still: he must be a perpetual exile for whom the earth will not even yield thorns and thistles, a resident of the land of Nod, of "wandering." Abraham enters the promised land only to leave it immediately for Egypt—where he succumbs at once to a moral compromise in which his wife's body is bartered for his own security. The same thing happens soon after in the land of Gerar—of "estrangement" or "temporary dwelling"—and will recur there in the story of Isaac and his wife, Rebekah. Jacob's daughter Dinah is raped by the local Canaanite chieftain, who then—having fallen in love—proposes marriage, trading relations, in a word: assimilation— a fate which the Israelites escape only by guile, murder, and flight. Finally, at the end of the book, the original court Jew, Joseph, survives one "pit" after another thanks to the divine blessing which shines upon him. He serves earthly lords and the Lord in Heaven in a way no native-born Egyptian and no Israelite living in the land of Israel ever could. The Jewish situation during centuries of wandering seems foretold in prescient detail. Neither Jew nor Gentile nor God escapes responsibility or critique.

But there is more: these stories are not merely Jewish (and human) nightmare but equally, often simultaneously, Jewish (and human) dream. There is greatness in the characters and purpose to the collective project on which they launch the children of Israel. Adam and Eve, the story tells us, could not handle their immense blessing. The generations leading up to Noah proved *de*generations. God could not keep sending floods to destroy the corruption visited upon the earth by the frail mortals whom God has made all-too-human. Instead God turns to the liberal solution: education. God will choose a people, teach them to walk God's way rather than follow their own untutored mixture of good and evil inclinations, give them perfect laws, and endow them with an abundant land over which these laws will hold sway while God protects them from external enemies. Perhaps humanity as a whole will thereby learn, in the long run, from this people's example.

That is why the text slows down when it reaches Abraham and his immediate descendants. It must deliberately and painfully educate them and us in the realities of Israelite responsibility. We too have to struggle with our families, our circumstances, and with God, in order to become Israel: "God-wrestlers." Jews are those who read of the injury to Jacob's thigh, and centuries later—imagine: as a consequence of a story!—alter what they will and will not eat.

Jacob's complex and not always likeable character points to the final—and perhaps the most potent—source of the Torah's enduring hold upon its readers: psychological acuity, never more evident than in Genesis. We seem to know these characters and the moves they make by heart, even before we have first met them. Women, Jewish and Gentile, have in recent decades poured forth a torrent of wonderful feminist midrash that takes readers inside female characters such as Miriam and Sarah. If we are men, the forefathers' dilemmas and betrayals seem preimprinted on our psyches. Male or female, Jew or non-Jew, we readily find ourselves at home in the biblical tale, understand the politics, know the personal wounds from the inside, bear the scars. We have perhaps also experienced the healing, assisted by our reading about it.

This was all the more true in my case, for I have a father whose Hebrew name is Abraham, and I knew even as a child that my father, although born in America, was (like the biblical Abraham) an immigrant of sorts, which made me the son of an immigrant. His parents had left absolutely everything behind them in the old country, but he too, though Philadelphia born and bred, had repeatedly crossed into new worlds barely explored and had left much behind him in the process, most notably his name. Abraham became Alan at some point in his youth. Eisenstein gave way to Eisen. The depression took away my father's not unrealistic dreams of concert halls (he won a state piano competition at sixteen, I am proud to report), and Al Eisen became a salesman in Gentile America.

My father woke up early in the morning, got in his Plymouth, and drove to call on superintendents of golf courses, not one of whom was ever a Jew. He went to sell them wetting agents and bottles of stuff that made the grass grow green. Sometimes I went along—cowering but curious in the car, or coaxed out to the shed: a little Isaac watching his father negotiating with the servants of Avimelekh, ruler of Gentiles. I hoped against hope they would laugh at his jokes and buy his products, so that we could go home safely (and more richly) to our tent. That was how it always happened with Abraham in the Bible. I knew too that my father had decided that not he but "his son, his only son, whom he loved," would master the new world's ways sufficiently to feel at home in it. This Abraham, like the original, would live through his seed.

I never believed that Abraham, who loved his son so, actually went up the mountain with the asses and the firewood and the servant boys—and Isaac—intending to sacrifice his "only son" (Ishmael didn't count) on the summit at God's command. I knew even in moments of hot Oedipal anger, when any excuse to hate him would have been welcome, that my father wouldn't have done such a thing. Nor had I ever experienced God or Judaism as hungry for such sacrifice of life. So I couldn't possibly read the text that way. Abraham had not left his homeland, contended with Pharaoh, argued over Sodom and Gomorrah, etc. etc.—all in accord with the will of his inscrutable God—just to lose his blessing, his future, his Isaac, in a barbaric act of slaughter. His God, whatever else He was, simply would not be that petty. Nor was He that trite. This God well knew the plots that entertained ancient Near Eastern divinities and had entirely new story lines in mind.

Abraham was not lying or indulging in mere wish when he assured the servant boys in Isaac's presence as he and his son left for the mountain that "we will return to you." By chapter 22 he had grown somewhat wise in the ways of his Lord. I see him waiting with one ear cocked for the angel's call all the while he saddles the asses, climbs the mountain, binds the cords, and lifts the knife. He knows the call will come, as of course it does in the end. We humans often have tests we do not need, and Abraham—more intimate with God than most of us—had long before this learned to endure them.

My own father Abraham, for example, had nearly lost his life to illness as a teenager. As an adult he and my mother had both become well acquainted with God's other angel, the one who does not come to save. But they had nonetheless maintained a kind of gut faith in God as well as in life, and have transmitted it to me. For all my years of wanderings, I have in this, as in other respects, ended up more like them than I ever cared in youth to acknowledge. Not that my path is mere imitation, or has lacked its determined rebellion. The son in me has always imagined Isaac in partial revolt against his sacrificing father and his father's frightening God. In this Isaac was perhaps aided and abetted by his mother—who, though she kept the home kosher, never quite forgave Abraham for the trip to Mount Moriah that morning and looked to her son to make worthwhile the larger journey on which, at her husband's urging, she had embarked.

Sarah is of course nearly silent in the biblical account: enraged perhaps at the treatment she received, at the instigation of her husband, in the courts of Pharaoh and Avimelekh. She does little more than banish Hagar in jealousy of her son's prerogatives and laugh when the angels tell her she will conceive in her old age. Yet I always imagined Sarah as quite a power in her own right. I thought I knew her quite well, from countless conversations in my mother's kitchen while Abraham was busy with other things, withdrawn into himself, or watching TV. Sarah not only laughed at God and life but interpreted them for her son—in part through her very laughter and her infinite love for him.

So when all is said and done, you see, I dig my parents' wells (as Genesis put it), or rather I dig my own—only to discover as Isaac did that my parents as often as not have dug them long before me. This is, I take it, the root meaning of tradition: "that which is passed on"— not a content, not specifics of behavior, but a path, a set of memories, a discipline inside which one finds freedom. The story into which I have followed my parents is not without its beauties—or its fear and trembling. I think I understand now, as an adult, why Isaac clung for dear life to more tangible goods than faith: Rebekah, whom he loved dearly, the children she bore him, the venison she cooked, and the tent and flocks he acquired among the servants of Avimelekh. I understand too, I think, why American Jews of my parents' generation put so much effort into securing the acceptance and the success which later came to seem so hollow to their children. They were well acquainted with the terrors of Jewish history in this century and were determined not to suffer them in America. The material successes which they achieved thanks to the American dream have been driven in part by nightmares.

No less important, these very successes offer Jews at century's end—heirs to the dreamers—an opportunity for Jewish growth that would not be possible had previous generations not bequeathed us the gift of America's embrace. Understanding leads to tolerance, the text teaches, and can promote growth. At the very end of Genesis, we see Joseph finally accept his father (with whom he had long been out of contact) for who and what he is. Joseph knows the family story, has relived it himself, and has added many chapters to it for better and for worse. He has taken on his inherited tradition—and so stands prepared to accept its ever-ambiguous blessing.

Reinterpreting Tradition

Many contemporary American Jews, I believe, now find themselves ready to take the step into—or further into—their tradition. They have come to understand, in part through study of Genesis, that the first question facing them is not *what they believe* but *where they will stand* in relation to the Jewish past. They know that Judaism is a commitment, not a creed, and that the key to revitalizing Jewish communities and eliciting Jewish commitment therefore lies in stimulating a live relation with the aspects of our inheritance that speak with "inner power." Some Jews feel this address in politics, or the arts. Others hear it in prayer or study. Still others establish a strong relation to tradition primarily through ritual observance or projects of social justice.

It is clear by this point in the nineties—well into the process of Jewish return and renewal—that the future of the Jewish story in this diverse society depends on how the varieties of Jews bring the tradition to life by making it part of their lives. Torah will grow through the range of concepts and emotions with which Jews animate their reading, the activities which flow from it, the concerns on which they bring the tradition to bear.

This brings us to the question which for me is the most important and difficult issue we face in taking on our tradition: the limits of legitimate innovation. We *must* alter what we inherit, to make it live in us, for us, and through us. That much is clear. But we cannot call the outcome of this project Torah, or even Jewish, just because Jews have conducted it. How then can we know that we are *authentically* carrying on what has been transmitted to us—and not merely constructing something new out of whole cloth, creating Judaism in our own image, and the image of our times?

Asking this question, we are in good company. The German Jewish thinker Franz Rosenzweig posed it in the 1920s in a letter to Martin Buber that has greatly influenced me and many others concerned with the problem in America.[12] Buber's antipathy to Jewish ritual and Jewish law, Rosenzweig complained, had left the Torah's crucial question of "what are we to do" in "the shackles put upon it . . . by the nineteenth century." One such "shackle" was the classical Reform position, which said: we know something is Jewish if it builds upon and furthers the "essential nature of Judaism" as conceived by some classical Reform thinkers—"ethical monotheism." If a practice fostered ethical behavior and/or belief in one God, it was essential and should be retained. If not, it could and should be dropped. This view gets us nowhere, Rosenzweig argued. He was right. It leaves us with a generic sort of Judaism shorn of all which makes it rich, deep, and distinctive.

The opposite view—no less a shackle—maintained that Judaism was what it had "always" been: the 613 commandments of the Torah as explicated by Orthodoxy. A practice was authentically Jewish if and only if it appeared in, or could be derived from, authoritative codes such as the Shulhan Arukh. This too was an unsatisfactory criterion to Rosenzweig, as it is to me. It allows too little room for maneuver, precludes the adaptations required to make the tradition live for the masses of Jews participating fully in the society and culture of the time. How then *shall* we judge the limits of interpretation? What "is this way to the Law," to Torah? How does one leap from "path"—all that Judaism has been and meant until now—to that which it must be in the very different circumstances that hold in every present and every future, which Rosenzweig called "pathlessness"?

Rosenzweig's answer was that only a "laborious and aimless detour through knowable Judaism gives us the certainty that the ultimate leap, from that which we know to that which we need to know at any price, the leap to the teachings, leads to *Jewish* teachings." I like this formulation. It means that we must inform ourselves as thoroughly as we can about how Jews in the past have made Torah matter in their lives. The library of texts is vast. The record of history is complex. Jews did not live or read Torah in only one way. Hence the need for "laborious" preparation. Nor can we act authentically if we decide in advance what we need to find when we turn to the Jewish past—a certain position on abortion or on welfare policy, a particular theory of creation or gender difference—and then rummage through the tradition until we find it, at which point we triumphantly pronounce our own position Judaism. Our search must rather be "aimless."

No one can say how much Jewish learning or doing is sufficient to satisfy this criterion. The goal always lies "a step beyond." But people generally know when they are being serious and when they are not. And one has to have confidence that Jews who have been serious enough to take the pains Rosenzweig described, who have become thoroughly informed by and about their tradition, can be trusted to act and teach in a way that authentically carries the tradition forward. If they cannot be trusted to do that, the tradition has no guarantee of survival in any case. For there is not and never has been any other way to carry given texts, sensibilities, and practices into new cultures and conditions.

Gershom Scholem, a great historian of Jewish mysticism and one of many German Jewish intellectuals who was profoundly influenced by Rosenzweig, cited two rabbinic reflections on the issue of "Revelation and Tradition" that have since appeared in virtually every work of contemporary Jewish thought dealing with the subject.[13] They are to my mind of invaluable importance. In the first story, God sets Moses down in the yeshiva of Rabbi Akiba (a prominent sage of the second century C.E.)—where he understands not a single word of the discussion proceeding in his name. The rabbis (or at least the author of this tale) apparently knew full well that Moses, not knowing Greek or Latin, not having witnessed either life in the Land of Israel or the destruction of the first and second Temples, not sharing the million and one cultural assumptions which informed their work of commentary, could not possibly make sense of the interpretations they gave his Torah. Yet they believed he wrote the words that facilitated or even demanded the very interpretations he could not comprehend.

In the second story a group of rabbis are engaged in debate over whether or not a certain oven is subject to impurity. All but Rabbi Eliezer are lined up on one side of the argument, which leads Eliezer in desperation to ask the stream of water by the building to prove his case by flowing backward (it does), the carob tree outside the window to support him by uprooting itself (it does), and the schoolhouse walls to totter (they do). But when he asks the intervention of a voice from heaven, and it comes, Rabbi Joshua rebukes God with a suitable quote from Deuteronomy—"it is not in heaven," i.e., the Torah no longer belongs to God but to human beings. They, not God, will henceforth interpret it. At the conclusion of the story another rabbi asks the prophet Elijah what God was doing in heaven while the debate between Eliezer and the others was proceeding. The answer? "God smiled and said, 'My children have defeated me. My children have defeated me.'" God wants what all parents want from their children when all is said and done: not to live as they did, but to walk in their path, to argue seriously over the meaning of their teachings.

The legitimacy of innovation, then, is not in doubt in this tradition. The need for the leap from path to pathlessness is clear. The requirement of a "laborious and aimless detour" such as the rabbis performed daily is apparent. But how can we in contemporary America *operationalize* this process? What specifics must be in place for us to do it—enabling us to proceed with confidence that the path we are walking is indeed Torah? What for example (to take a concrete case transpiring before our eyes) ensures that a Jewish feminist transformation of tradition is really Jewish?[14]

I want to suggest, as my concluding reflection on the matter of "taking on tradition," five formal criteria which should guide us. I call them "formal" because they refer to the *process* of our innovation rather than the *content* which results from it, though content will of course be shaped by process, and at times determined by it. I derive all five from Rosenzweig's teaching, playing Akiba, as it were, to his Moses. They shall be mentioned here very briefly and not defended or explained. Each will be explored at length in the chapters which follow—as they are, I believe, in the remaining four books of the Torah.

1. *Learning.* We cannot take the tradition into our lives unless we have made it ours through study and performance. Our children will not be able to make choices other than ours, will never have different texts or practices speak to them with "inner power," unless we transmit more than what has proven most compelling to us. The learning must be broad and deep if authentic selection and interpretation are to occur. A feminist Judaism must be learned in both feminist and in Jewish sources to make a claim to authenticity. Appeals to "the traditional Jewish concern for justice" or other generalities will not do.

2. *Community.* Tradition is not received or adapted or transmitted in isolation. I cannot convincingly explain the importance of a Jewish ritual or text to my children if mine is the only house in the neighborhood that pays attention to it. Were Judaism only a set of teachings to be read for purposes of individual enlightenment, people

could perhaps absorb the books all by themselves, with the help of other books (or teachers) that interpret them. But Torah is a tradition, to be lived, in the real world of the everyday. That is one reason why Judaism is intimately involved with family, and until the modern period could not be separated from any aspect of everyday life. Each Jew needs a Jewish community in order to fulfill the Torah's teaching—and beyond that community, needs the wider social and political worlds in which the Torah must likewise be reflected upon and made effective.

That is so in at least two senses. Jewish commitment demands acts of justice and compassion that intrinsically involve life among other people for whom we share responsibility. And Jewish ethics—the rights and wrongs of Torah, applied to our situation—emerge only from communities that ponder pressing dilemmas together in dialogue with their tradition. We will never succeed in revitalizing Judaism in this country unless we can re-create and sustain engaged communities of Jews, people who trust one another to say: I think you are wrong about this, I confess I have been wrong about that. Jewish feminism is emerging from just such communities of women (and in some cases men) committed to negotiating difficult new terrain together.

3. *Time and space.* Neither traditions nor communities can survive, let alone flourish, without the existence of times and spaces that they define as well as inhabit. If there is only Saturday and not Shabbat, or Christmas but not Hanukkah; if September marks only the start of the academic year, but we lack Tishre, the season of the High Holy Days; if Judaism finds expression only in the private spaces of home and synagogue but not in the streets, the arts, the media of American society more generally, it will remain a shadow of what it once was and might again become in our day. America cannot provide what Israel does in terms of Jewish time and public Jewish space. We for the most part move to non-Jewish rhythms. The neighborhoods in which most Jews live do not and will not resemble the segregated Hasidic areas of Brooklyn. But we must have potent Jewish times and vibrant Jewish spaces, or Torah will not live among us. The creation of such frameworks (in large part through ritual) has been one of the most challenging tasks facing Jewish feminists, as it has been for contemporary American Jewry as a whole.

4. *Language and grammar.* Traditions and communities also need their own languages, both literal and figurative, as well as "grammars" that specify how to put those languages into practice. This is a commonplace of anthropology. The words we speak reflect and shape the concepts in our minds. Certain things will not occur to us because we do not have the language to describe them. Words can conversely call experience into being, just as God's word did in the Beginning. Every Jewish community until our own has had a Jewish language in addition to the language of its surroundings—usually Hebrew as well as a dialect such as Yiddish or Ladino. Most American Jews have neither the one nor the other, and it has affected their ability to think and act authentically as Jews.

The implications are clear. Those who can learn Hebrew should be strongly urged to do so; those who do not should avail themselves of the growing library of Jewish literature in translation. But figurative language—basic "cultural literacy"—is indispensable. A Jew has to know why *tzedakah* is not adequately rendered as "charity," what it means to "do a mitzvah" or "be a mentsch," why the passion for social justice is an integral part of the grammar of Jewish commitment, why politics and education have been fundamental concerns of Judaism from the books of Numbers and Deuteronomy onward. Jewish men and women must know these things not in the way any New Yorker knows a few words of Yiddish but from personal experience, from the inside, from practice.

5. Finally, and most controversially, there is *God.* I have emphasized that the encounter with tradition does not start or end with God, that it always has encompassed far more than God, and always will. Indeed, I have urged (following Buber) that in the first instance Jews suspend their problems with God as they draw near to the Torah and the tradition more generally. But the question of God must be faced sooner or later if we seek continuity with our tradition, because every strand in that tradition takes it—takes God—seriously. The ancestors were not all believers, and we won't be either: whether because of the Holocaust, modernity, feminism, or the givens of the human condition. Previous generations held to faith in a hundred different conceptions of God—and at times some Jews probably doubted all of them. We will likely develop conceptions of which they had no knowledge, and some of us may doubt them all the more.

Continuity with tradition, now as ever, does not demand constant belief, and certainly not adherence to any particular conception of God.

But encounter with Torah necessarily involves *wrestling* with the Ultimate. This is what makes us Israel. For a Jewish community as a whole to renounce the struggle as adolescent or anachronistic is to break the chain of continuity with tradition and to dismiss the "ultimate concern" of our ancestors as delusion. Militantly secular Israelis of the past century are the exception which proves this rule. Their rebellion against the God of Israel was necessary to return the people of Israel to the Land of Israel—and has facilitated the rejuvenation of the Torah of Israel. As a rule, however, God-wrestling is a Jewish imperative that cannot be brooked. The task is thankfully well underway among Jewish feminists, and is being pursued with increasing profundity elsewhere in the American Jewish community as well. It can be undertaken only through common but individual quest and searching: if not in youth, then in old age; if not this year, then next; if not in one person's life, then in that of his children, her friends; if not with this face of God, then with another of the Infinite that Jews have encountered.

My ideal vision of the American Jewish community, then, would include *many* and *diverse* communities of Jews, each composed of individuals bound up in tangible obligation with one another and engaged in serious dialogue with Jewish tradition. We need multiple tables at which Torah is studied, varied constructions of Jewish times and spaces, a plurality of inflections to the language and grammar bequeathed to us, and the gift of struggles with God (the Ultimate, the Transcendent) as different from one another as those of Abraham and Isaac, or Abraham and Sarah, or Sarah and Miriam. If these five elements were in place among a critical mass of American Jews, and if they figured prominently in the Jewish identity held out to the thousands upon thousands of Jews who at any given moment are taking their first tentative steps toward further involvement with their tradition, there would be every reason for confidence in American Jewry's leap from path to pathlessness. Our teachings would take their place in the continuing development of Torah; our generation's role in the continuity of Judaism's never-ending story would be assured.

2

⤜∞⤛

Exodus

HISTORY, FAITH, AND COVENANT

At the start of the Torah's second book, we face an interpretive problem comparable to the problem that—following Rashi, who followed Rabbi Isaac—we encountered at the Beginning. Why are we *still* not ready for Sinai? Why the long, drawn-out story of Israel's enslavement and redemption, including the decrees of the Pharaoh, the birth and calling of the liberator, God's infliction of ten plagues on Egypt, the miraculous crossing of the Red Sea? Why only then, in chapter 19, do we and the Israelites finally arrive at the wilderness beneath the sacred mountain?

One cannot explain the necessity of this history from God's point of view (the text itself does not try), or even from that of the author of Exodus (who has to respect God's silence on the point). Nor do we know (or need to know, I think) if the events described in the book actually took place. Their meaning does not depend on that. What we *do* need to understand—so as to find this meaning—is why it is important for Jews in every generation, including our own, to read the Exodus story year after year. The problem to be addressed, in other words, is not ancient Israel's preparation for Sinai, but our own. And here too, as in Genesis, the structure of the Torah itself seems to provide an answer.

It does so, I think, by once again addressing the situation of its readers. We have already seen that the "right to make promises," as Nietzsche called it,[1] requires coming to terms with the facts of *personal biography,* understanding who the "I" is who will have to stand by his or her words. No less, however, adult commitment entails coming to terms with the facts of *collective history.* Our options, while substantial, are not unlimited. However much we would like to promise, our ability to fulfill commitments is always constrained. For the most part the limits are not of our creation but rather a function of the situation into which we are born and in which we must act. The "covenant of fate," in Rabbi Joseph Soloveitchik's phrase, binds us *involuntarily* long before we undertake the "covenant of destiny," which can and must *be chosen.* The latter can be realized only in (and often despite) the conditions dictated by the former, indeed is often directed at transforming them.[2]

Until we face up to history, then, attend to its inexorable demands, understand the time and place into which we are called to act, we are not ready for mature promises to each other or to God. Both sorts of covenant—enacted simultaneously by the Israelites at Sinai—are difficult in the best of circumstances. Hence the text's instruction, in the first part of Exodus, to get ready.

We too require such preparation. I have already described the resistance among contemporary Americans, Jewish or Gentile, to covenants which bind us firmly to one another with or without our consent. Curtailment of autonomy is strenuously opposed in our society. We go to great lengths to keep all our options open. And that is all the more true of commitment to God, a kind of covenant which for many of our generation is literally out of the question. How could it be otherwise? Once God was a presence in daily life for Jews and Gentiles alike: a friend or provider, a parent or master (all favorite images in classical Jewish sources). For some Jews that is still the case. A friend of mine, who grew up Orthodox in Jerusalem, reports that he could find God as a child every time he looked in the refrigerator. God was a presence as reliable as the little light that goes on when the door opens—perhaps because the meat and dairy inside were strictly separated, the "Provider to all" was thanked at every meal, and the street in front of my friend's house was closed to traffic every Friday before sunset to prevent the desecration of the Sabbath.

Most contemporary American Jews did not grow up that way— and even if they did God has likely become, by the time of their adulthood, at best a distant Creator or inscrutable Judge, at worst a childish fiction which has long since been outgrown. God figures in many Jewish imaginations as a "deity" who takes up residence in the mind only as an intellectual problem and speaks rarely if at all to the heart. Such promptings as we do receive—"signals of the transcendent," Peter Berger calls them; glimpses of the ultimate; turns toward God in moments of crisis or exultation—are generally filed away somewhere in consciousness, perhaps to protect them all the better from reason's chilling gaze. God is not the "abiding presence" found in sacred stories and the prayerbook, and is therefore not a conceivable partner for a relationship, which by definition must be ongoing.

Nor is God's absence entirely regretted, even by many who do believe, or the distance separating God from humanity one which most of us are eager to overcome. Adulthood requires a measure of independence, after all. Parental supervision is rarely the best condition for mature achievement. How could we practice history or science if these were subject to outside interference? What could we know? How much could we accomplish?

It is no wonder, given this context for the reading of the Torah, that the text's claim for God's presence at a real mountain on a certain day in a given calendar year before people like you and me cannot elicit widespread belief. Still less can such a text command widespread obedience—a response which does not come in the theoretical realm where faith is often found but belongs rather to the world of practical concern that includes things like love and parenting, the pursuit of our professions and the maintenance of our societies. The relationship with God, which to the Torah matters more than anything else ever could, has become in our culture a matter about which we simply need never decide. God rarely arises as a subject in adult living rooms. Even the sermons in many a synagogue have for decades avoided it assiduously.

This is not healthy for a community committed by its tradition to God-wrestling. Nor, I am convinced, is it irreparable. "God-talk" seems to be experiencing a revival among American Jews of late. Adults of the current generation seem more inclined than their elders to trust their encounters with transcendence, to follow the "signals" even if they lead beyond reason's capacity to follow. My aim in this chapter is to facilitate that stretch toward faith and covenant among contemporary American Jews by directing attention to the helpful framing of these matters provided in the Book of Exodus.

Two aspects of that framing are especially important: first, the insistence that God be known—and eventually loved—with "heart and soul and might," which means through intellect as well as emotion, using a combination of reason, tradition, and experience; and, second, the grounding of faith and covenant in the stuff of lived history. That is where, according to the master Jewish story, the encounter with ultimacy is meant to occur—and where, for many Jews today, the events of the past half century have erected a barrier to faith which is too high to leap over and too wide to get round.

Let me say once again before proceeding that I do not believe the revitalization of Jewish community and commitment requires either "belief in God" or submission to the authority of divine commandments. One can be a member in good standing of the Jewish community without these commitments, and they cannot in any case be produced on demand, divine or human. I am persuaded, however, that American Jewry needs to take part *as a community*, in a way it has not in recent generations, in the conversation regarding faith and covenant begun by Israel (according to our people's master-story) at Sinai. While there is more than one way to carry on that conversation—indeed the Torah itself, as we shall see, provides multiple points of entry and varied modes of participation—*God-wrestling* constitutes a condition for the very existence of the conversation that seems non-negotiable. And two other things are required as well.

One is a renewed sense of *communal obligation*. It need not depend on acceptance of the authority of Jewish law, certainly not in its present Orthodox forms. But we do need to revive the notion of *mitzvah*: distinctive behaviors performed by Jews individually and collectively—in a variety of ways, to be sure—because it is right for Jews to do so; because it is what Jews do.

The other requirement is that, though we continue to "hear the voice of Sinai" differently, we agree that the covenant summons us to *work in and on the world*. Standing at Sinai means not only facing up to history but working to transform it. Jews, whatever sort of Jews they are, have no choice but to join in this task. Membership in the covenant demands that we accept our share of responsibility, as recipients of Torah, for repair of the world.

Will we all ever agree to do so, or agree on what it would mean? Of course not. But that is not the issue. The Israelites of old were certainly no less contentious than contemporary American Jews when it comes to arguing over the terms of the covenant, let alone living up to them. But they, and all subsequent generations of Jews until about a century ago, were united by their very argument "for the sake of Heaven" over what it means to observe and preserve Torah. *That* is the dispute more worth having than any other, in my view. It is the conversation to which I hope to contribute here.

Facing History

The parallels between ancient Israelites and ourselves in respect to the demands of history are striking—far more so, in fact, than most of us would wish. Like us, the Children of Israel faced (and had to face down) a reality that was nothing short of terrifying. Pharaoh tried to erase their existence, and in a variety of ways—culminating at the Sea—attempted to block the Israelites' path to Sinai. Hitler came dangerously close a mere half century ago to annihilating the Jews, killing many of our own ancestors, relatives, and friends in the process. He still threatens, a half-century "after Auschwitz," to block Jewish journeys to God and goodness. The Israelites of course did manage with God's assistance to reach the place of faith and covenant, and if we too get there nonetheless, it is thanks in large part to the fact that we like they have been witness to a remarkable liberation. For me, as for many Jews of this generation, Jewish history has meant above all Holocaust and Israel. The latter does not justify the former. Israel can never make sense of the Holocaust, but it does help me to overcome its impact. Both have been crucial to the formation of my adult Jewish identity. They continue to loom large in the way I think about Sinai.

Exodus establishes our encounter with fateful history in its very first verses. Jacob's children have gone down to Egypt and rapidly become a nation, and we are immediately impelled at the narrator's direction to feel sympathy for the plight which has overtaken them and to identify with their future hero, Moses. Both Moses and the people are helpless at the outset. The latter are being victimized by an unjust tyrant. Their future leader is a baby lying in a basket on the Nile. And as Moses quickly grows tall in Pharaoh's court, and Israel's troubles mount, our anxiety as readers grows—as does our identification with the victims of Pharaoh's oppression. We too want to banish injustice from the world, to save our loved ones from distress. God's sins of commission and omission where human suffering is concerned stand in obvious need of correction. We would willingly offer ourselves for the task. When Moses strikes down the Egyptian taskmaster in chapter 2, after seeing him beat an Israelite slave, we are already prepared by multiple acts of identification to cheer him on—thereby accepting our share of complicity for what he has done.

This is odd, and quite remarkable: how can one, why would one, identify to this degree with a deed performed three millennia ago by a character perhaps fictional? Yet we do so, as per the text's intentions, assisted perhaps by Moses' "human-all-too-human" look around before he acts to make sure no one is watching. His righteous violence seems born of a native sense of human justice that we share, and his people represent the victims of oppression in every time and place, and therefore have a claim on us whether we are Jewish or not. Moses has done what we would wish to have done in similar circumstances. His act has moved him fatefully over a personal boundary line dividing Egyptian from Israelite, immaturity from destiny, and the text wants to take us with him. "Now you," it seems to say, addressing its readers. "It is your turn to move. Exit whatever Egypt afflicts you. Set yourself and others free from what enslaves you. Work to end the injustice of your world. Take on the responsibility you've been running from."

I don't think I could have fully appreciated the stark opening chapters of Exodus, their moral choices so clearly delineated, without the encounter with Holocaust and Israel. I certainly would not have felt the full force of Pharaoh's behavior. His initial warning to his nation concerning my ancestors is frightening: "Behold, this people, the Children of Israel, are too numerous and powerful for us. Let us deal wisely with him lest he multiply and, when war break out, he too will be counted among our enemies, and fight against us, and rise up from the land." It soon gets worse. "Dealing wisely" leads to an order that midwives kill male Israelite infants at birth, and when that policy fails, Pharaoh orders his entire people to cast male Israelite babies into the Nile. We are talking, in modern terms, about genocide. One nation sets about murdering another.

Readers who are so inclined can of course dismiss the decrees presented in the text as Israelite or Jewish ideology, constructed after the fact to rationalize God's drowning of Egypt's army in the sea and/ or (if that too is a mere fiction) the Israelite conquest of Canaanite territory, which Egypt at that time claimed. Pharaoh's order to kill the Israelites could also be seen as a plot device which sets in motion the chain of events resulting in the birth of a "holy nation." The king can be viewed as a mere puppet who helps to set the stage on which God—producer, director, and lead actor in this show—will enter history as Redeemer. I myself used to read Exodus this way—suspiciously, keeping my distance—before encountering the Holocaust, in Israel.

That encounter did not persuade me that the narrative is factually accurate. The Exodus story might well be a fiction. The sea might never have split, by miracle or tidal wave. The Israelites might or might not have been slaves for Pharaoh and freed. But genocide, as we all know by this point in the human story, *is* a fact. That cannot be doubted. Its origins perhaps go back even further than the Egypt of the Pharaohs. Nor did the barbarity of the Nazis suffice to bring genocide to an end. Its most recent objects have included Bosnian Muslims who were the victims of "ethnic cleansing" by Bosnian Serbs while the world at large (myself included) stood by and did nothing.

In the shadow of such events one has to pause at Pharaoh's political rhetoric in the first chapters of Exodus. A Jew in particular must take stock of the facts of the twentieth-century Jewish situation to which the king's words point. A sentence very similar to Exodus 1:22, ordaining the murder of my people, was uttered a little more than half a century ago by a leader who carried it out with brutal efficiency. Whatever one makes of the plagues and the sea turning into dry land, *that* part of the Exodus story has proved all too real and recurrent. And if the wonder at the sea did not happen this time around, as wondrous salvation failed to arrive on most of the occasions when it was most needed, that too has to figure in our reckoning. Experience of the world must always be brought to the reading of Torah. This century's history makes it far more difficult to read the opening chapters of Exodus with composure, and harder still to get through them and reach Sinai, which might well have proved a mountain difficult for moderns to scale in any event.

Israel has for me as for other Jews of this generation played a crucial role in this effort. The Jewish State has stood, during my entire adult life, at the very center of my identity, whereas the Holocaust, perhaps for reasons of biography, has never been at the forefront and is not today. Growing up in the fifties and early sixties, I like most American Jews at the time hardly ever heard the Holocaust mentioned. It was in my consciousness anyway, of course: not a topic of study or conversation, but a constant shadow in the near-distance of my mind. As a child it hit me with some force that I had been born a mere three years after Israel, and a mere six after the shutdown of the death camps. I took for granted, reading *The Diary of Anne Frank,* that nothing of my good fortune could ever be taken for granted. I could not assume that people were "basically good at heart," never underestimate the horrors we are capable of visiting upon one another. For I too might have been among the Holocaust's victims, and wondered whether, had I been a German, I would have had the courage to resist the Nazis' decrees.

It was in Israel that I first felt the full impact of the chronological coincidence linking me to the Jewish state as well as to Auschwitz, and linking them one to another; there too that I had my first nightmare featuring Nazis. One could not avoid the connection in the mid-seventies, when I first spent extended time in Israel. Survivors and their children made up a significant share of the population. Their stories were on TV, in the arts, in living rooms. Even now, when the Holocaust has reached the forefront of Jewish consciousness everywhere, its place in Israeli Jewish culture seems unique. A few years back, on sabbatical, I sat in the Jerusalem Cinemateque and watched a film called "Because of that War." It concerns (and stars) two leading Israeli rock musicians, both the children of Holocaust survivors. That background permeates their music, and the music, like the film, is searing. My immediate response when the lights came on was thanksgiving that I was able to encounter it in the original Hebrew, in Jerusalem. I knew its subject concerned me. This was my fate, these were my people. All the more important to have direct access to it and to them, without subtitles.

My second response, almost as immediate, was to affirm the centrality of Israel in contemporary Jewish history—still an issue of live debate between American Jews and Israelis these days, but which for me at that moment was resolved. The previous chapter of Jewish history ended at Auschwitz. Although America is not peripheral to what has followed, the main event, the gathering of what remains of the Jewish people after Hitler, the Jews' most defiant building of a collective future, is underway in Israel. One feels the continuity all the more powerfully because the threat to collective Jewish existence has not ended in the world's only state with a Jewish majority. Hence the nightmare, I suspect. It is a new and disturbing sensation for an American to be surrounded by so many people who would like one's own people removed, or dead.

All the more reason to be grateful for the reality awaiting one outside the Cinemateque: for the soldiers on the street, who furnish palpable protection; for the view of the Old City, symbol of Jewish survival despite enormous odds over three millennia; for the entire round of daily life, so intense that it requires every sensory organ to work overtime; for the fact—ever surprising to a diaspora Jew—that public space and public time are shaped in all their vitality by Judaism rather than by another tradition. It is a real pleasure to turn on the TV or radio and hear a Jewish language and debates over Jewish concerns.

Finally—and for me, at least, no small matter—there is the light. Sitting near the Western Wall, nearly blinded by the noonday sun, one shades one's eyes to stare up at the Temple Mount and is prompted by the searing brightness to reveries of Isaiah—who looked out some twenty-five hundred years ago from the courts of the Temple at these same barren mountains of Judea, which then too made their way down to an ever Dead Sea. No lush greenery in this vista. No rest under vines or fig trees. In Jerusalem's inexorable light one is reminded, as Isaiah was, that all of us stand between the hardness of rock below and the directness of sun above. Caught between sky and stone Isaiah could not boast or flee but only look into the depths of self which the light had penetrated and left exposed. From this his prophecy emerged, perhaps; from this blinding light he may have learned to see more clearly.

The lesson which the prophets of Israel saw and taught was not that nothing human matters but exactly the opposite. "Holy, holy, holy is the Lord of Hosts. The whole earth is full of His glory." Any reader of Hebrew can make out the words on the ancient Isaiah scroll, two thousand years old and more, on display at the Israel Museum. It is doubly hard to avoid the lesson, reading it in Jerusalem; the city itself discourages pursuits with which one ordinarily busies oneself in less penetrating light. The architecture of ultimate concern is everywhere: minarets and steeples, crosses and domes. So are the signs and anxieties of the eternal contest over who God is and what God wants. Anyone who would trivialize life in Jerusalem works against the grain. Normalcy is an effort, an ideology. Security, ever absent, is a slogan that wins elections. There is simply too much history about, perpetually calling one to attention.

American Jews must *choose* to direct their attention to history, Jewish or American, whereas Israelis know that the covenant of fate has already chosen them. Though bombs always claim their victims indiscriminately, and have recently begun to explode on American streets as well, Israeli Jews cannot escape the realization that they are, because they are Jews, almost always the intended targets. War and bloodshed intended to eliminate their presence are virtually unceasing. The covenant of fate is as a result self-evident. And the covenant of destiny is more apparent in Israel as well. When one rides a public bus and looks at the varied faces of the Jews on board, one realizes: so this is Jewish peoplehood, this is the place in the world where all Jews come together, to live and quarrel and manage their affairs in close proximity.

The perception—often forceful—perhaps accounts for the sense of homecoming reported by many American Jewish visitors, who cannot speak Hebrew, find the landscape and the food unfamiliar, and are disturbed by the lack of civility in ordinary human interactions, yet feel somehow at home. It is not just that sides have obviously been drawn up before they arrived, and like it or not they belong to one of them: the covenant of fate. Nor is it just the pride at collective achievement: the sight of blooming deserts, roads clogged with traffic, and immigrants who have been absorbed by the hundreds of thousands—the marks of collective Jewish action, the covenant of destiny. The point is that Jews are here, before one's eyes, not only individually but as a people. Hitler did not end the Jewish story. Life has in this instance at least defeated death. "Am Yisrael Chai"—the people of Israel lives.

That above all is the meaning of Israel for me, as it is perhaps for other American Jews. I know the reality of Israeli society, politics, and culture fairly well, but I treasure the place because its significance is mythic, larger than life, transparent to the depths of meaning. The two, myth and reality, are inextricably intertwined. I need Israel to exist—and it does, thank God. Its vitality so deeply satisfies me because vitality is, as it were, existence squared and magnified. Auschwitz, by coming so close, threatens my very being, as it literally threatened the existence of the people whom I most love in this world. Had my wife's maternal grandmother not been sent out of Poland in place of her brother, who was originally supposed to leave, my partner in life, the mother of my children, would never have been born.

But they were born, their voices fill my days with happiness, we are here to tell this tale. Judaism too lives. Torah still speaks—and, as Israel demonstrates, can actually matter in the world. That is true in America too, of course, but in Israel it is far more obvious. People argue over Torah endlessly, on television and in living rooms. They criticize each other mercilessly for failures to live up to its teachings, stone cars on the Sabbath in its name, perform surpassing acts of justice because God commanded them—and sometimes parade injustice as divine imperative, or reduce profundity to schmaltz and kitsch, and then with the very next breath prove capable of everyday kindnesses in the name of God that are far more valuable to me than profundity. The Holocaust too is not merely remembered but used as motivation for great effort, even heroism, even as it is all too often flung against anyone not of the speaker's political or religious persuasion. This is the price one pays for vitality. We find ourselves cursing the abuses to which Torah is subject, now that Jews have the power to commit them, and blessing the fact that this power is now ours, that life is ours, to use for good, to make Torah live.

Israel, then—even while it does not in any way "solve the problem of the Holocaust," does not compensate for it, does not close the wounds in Jewish psyches which half a century after Auschwitz have barely begun to harden into scar—can nonetheless help one to get around the awful history that threatens to block the path to Sinai. It does so by providing a graphic experience of the life opened up by covenant, a sense of what Jews can accomplish when fate and destiny are joined. And if that gift is effective, as it was in my case, it brings us face to face once more with the difficulties which Jews would likely have had with faith and covenant in any case, even had the Holocaust never occurred.

Relation to God is never a simple matter, as the Bible more than any other religious text makes clear. Faith always strains credulity and defies a great deal of experience. That is why it is called faith. And while the problems involved in relation to the Ultimate have been greatly exacerbated in the past two centuries, for reasons that need no further rehearsal here, chapter 19 of Exodus makes it clear that these problems are far from unique to moderns. The ancient Israelites faced at least some of them as well—a fact which, emphasized time and again in the text, may well help us too to get around them.

Accepting the Yoke of Covenant

We arrive at Sinai, at long last, "on the first day of the third month after leaving Egypt." The memories of Genesis's family stories are firmly in mind, and the historical experience of Jewish peoplehood is as close to us as flesh. Reason is not suspended as we camp at the foot of the mountain—indeed, as we shall see, it will be required to understand what transpires there—but wonderment at recent events is overwhelming, and serves for a time at least to challenge reason's unlimited sway. The Israelites are prepared to undertake new commitments, to step into a future that has only now come into view. And once again the text prepares us for what lies ahead by making it harder. A whole new set of challenges emerges.

Moses first goes up the mountain and comes down with a covenant that Israel is called upon to ratify in general terms. The people are to be "holy" to God (what this means, apart from the root connotation of apartness, is not clear), separated among the nations as priests are distinguished within each individual people. The Israelites agree to these terms without hesitation, reasoning perhaps that they could negotiate the precise degree of exclusivity, and the details of their national vocation, later on. So far so good. They send Moses back to God bearing news of their unanimous consent. "All that the Lord has spoken we will obey."

God then announces an unprecedented visitation. "And the Lord said to Moses: I will come to you in a thick cloud, in order that the people may hear when I speak with you and so trust in you ever after." In three days, after Moses has gotten the people ready, "YHWH will descend before the eyes of all the people on Mount Sinai."

This is striking; the purpose of the event at hand is not to reveal God in any way, shape, or form but to establish the authority of God's prophet, Moses. God is coming to "you," will speak with "you," so that Israel will trust in "you"—all in second person singular. But what follows is more astounding still. Moses returns down the mountain with the message of God's imminent descent. We get ready.

And, on the third day, at morning, there were thunders [*kolot*] and lightnings and a heavy cloud on the mountain, and the sound [*kol*] of a shofar very strong and all the people trembled in the camp. And Moses went forth from [or: with] the people to meet God outside the camp, and they stood at the foot of the mountain. And Mount Sinai was all smoke because YHWH had descended on it in fire, and the smoke rose like the smoke of a furnace and the mountain trembled greatly. And the *kol* of the shofar grew stronger and stronger. Moses would speak, and God would answer in a *kol*. And YHWH descended on Mount Sinai to the top [literally: head] of the mountain, and YHWH called Moses to the head of the mountain, and Moses went up. [Exodus 19:16–20]

Now we really are ready, or so we think. The prose has built to just this moment. The mountain and the people are both quaking. By now we are not surprised that the so-called appearance of God before our very eyes is wrapped in layer upon layer of concealment. We stand below at the bottom of the mountain, having sent Moses above to the summit, and the entire mountain is covered in cloud. We know God is there, but we cannot see God. Nor will God's voice come through directly: the text has deliberately told us of the *kol* of the thunders and the *kol* of the shofar. What exactly will be heard below when Moses speaks to God, and God answers him in a *kol*? We are about to find out.

Yet God is apparently not yet satisfied with the arrangements. "Get down, warn the people, lest they break through to YHWH, to see, and many of them fall. And let the priests who approach to YHWH sanctify themselves. Lest YHWH break forth among them." Moses, not for the last time, is uncomprehending. "But the people cannot go up to Mount Sinai, because You already warned us saying, 'make the mountain off-limits, and sanctify it.'" God will have none of this. "*Lekh red*"—two short imperatives—"get down, and come up, you and Aaron with you, and the elders and the people, let them not burst through to ascend to YHWH lest He break forth among them." So "Moses went down to the people and said to them. . . ."

Said what? Presumably, fulfilling his role as message-carrier between God and Israel, Moses transmitted God's final warning. But the text of chapter 19 ends with the words "and he said to them," and resumes in chapter 20 with the Ten Commandments: the content of

the so-called revelation for which all of chapter 19 had been preparation! To compound the confusion, Moses apparently emerges from
the preparatory chapter (as do we) standing at *the bottom* of the
mountain. We are not told by the text that he has ascended again in
order to receive God's word. Above and below, despite the attempts
at barrier construction and the high rhetorical drama, are not clearly
delimited. Moses goes up and down repeatedly. God is above and we
are below. Yet God has descended. And we, within certain limits, can
go up. The experience of God's presence transforms and transcends
the usual categories. The very first words of the text following the
tenth commandment will confirm this. "And all the people, seeing
the *kolot* and the lightnings and the *kol* of the shofar and the
mountain of smoke, when the people saw this they fell back and stood
at a distance." In ordinary experience we do not see the sound of
thunder or shofar. But Sinai, of course, is no ordinary experience. Just
what, then, are we to make of it?

The text itself, I think, by its elisions, confusions, and omissions,
guarantees that there is no *one* thing which we *can* make of it. The
seventy nations of the world, the rabbis theorized, all received the
Torah, not just Israel. God's word was sent forth in seventy languages, so that every member of every culture could understand. Even
among the Israelites, one midrash insists, every person heard it
somewhat differently. These textual possibilities, seized on by the
rabbis, are perhaps the single most important gift of Torah, contained
in the very manner of its giving. The text *must* speak to all of us, if
God's declared intentions are to prove effective, and it must therefore
speak to us as the people we are. Different individuals will inevitably
hear it differently, bring different needs and talents to the hearing,
approach Torah from a number of different angles.

Two of those approaches—both encouraged by the chapters in
Exodus just reviewed—seem to me of particular importance to the
present generation of Jews. They might be called coming at Torah
from our side and *from God's side*. We have already noted that the
covenant given at Sinai simultaneously bound the Israelites to one

another and to God. They not only became a holy people at Sinai, but a *people*, full stop. They were a *kingdom*—a political entity, capable of collective action—only by virtue of consecration as a kingdom of priests. The rabbis long ago observed further that the Ten Commandments are inscribed on two tablets rather than one, suggesting a division between the first five, which govern relations *between human beings and God,* and the second five, which govern relations *between one human being and another.* Building on this, I think that we can usefully view the two tablets as complementary understandings of Sinai: different paths of access for different sorts of contemporary Jews.

One can come to Sinai from "our side" of the relationship. God need not figure in the decision, at least not at the outset. One might simply want to stand as a Jew with the Jewish people: to live and perpetuate its culture, serve universal ideals as it has formulated them, find meaning for oneself and transmit it to one's children inside the "never-ending story" and "pattern for living" which have not only sustained Jews for centuries but have perhaps constituted the Jewish people's greatest gifts to humanity as a whole. Three steps are involved in this journey "from our side" to Sinai.

The obligations involved in such a covenant begin with the fundamental ethical behaviors enforced by every known social order, set forth by the Torah in chapter 20 of Exodus in the name of God and morality alike. Respect your parents. Do not murder, steal, or commit adultery. No false witness or lustful encroachment on the domain of others. (I follow Maimonides' reading of "Thou shalt not covet" as a prohibition on behavior rather than desire.) It is no wonder that six of the ten commandments are devoted to these ethical principles. Honoring parents provides a bridge between obligations to our proximate creators and duty to the ultimate Creator of all things. The commands enforce a social contract that is very nearly universal because it is basic to every societal arrangement. God need not be invoked to justify the contemporary acceptance of such obligations, though to the Torah the separation between the "Judge of all the World" and justice is of course unthinkable. We can undertake these obligations on other grounds.

The second step in this approach is to recognize that we do not live simply as human beings in general, or only as members of a particular society such as America, bound to its laws by implicit social contract. "Our side" also includes the dense frameworks for life that we moderns normally separate out as culture or community but which in Jewish tradition are wrapped up in God's design for Israel. All of us start life in a family and a local community of some sort, as well as a nation. These frameworks inevitably carry and generate obligations as they (hopefully) endow us, and sustain us, with meaning. The Torah presumes, in agreement with the communitarian philosopher Michael Sandel, that the term "community" connotes

> allegiances [that] go beyond the obligations I voluntarily incur and the "natural duties" I owe to human beings as such. . . . To some I owe more than justice requires or even permits . . . in virtue of those more or less enduring attachments and commitments which taken together partly define the person I am.[3]

The choices we make as we go through life build on those presented to us before we choose, and our choices come with further obligations in tow. We have special responsibilities to family, friends, and community, and find meaning in and through those relations as well as through the exercise of the responsibilities which flow from them. If all works as it should, the grudging performance of mere duty is transformed over time into enthusiastic acts of love. All of us recognize obligations of this sort, I think, and regularly respond to them. "All Jews are responsible to one another," as the Talmud puts it, because all share membership in the same extended family or community, emerge from the same history, are subject to the same fate, and derive meaning from the same story and "patterns for living" which they by common effort maintain.

The third and final step in the approach to Sinai's covenant "from our side" is the recognition that communities survive and thrive not merely physically but spiritually. Judaism—for two thousand years a diaspora community exclusively, and still faced with the challenge of minority existence in America—can continue only if its ideals and culture are transmitted in a form that is compelling to successive generations. If one is committed to Jewish survival, one must pledge fealty as well to the means required to secure it: festivals and dietary laws, rites, and symbols. Many Jews light candles on Friday evening or attend Passover seders or attend synagogue in precisely this spirit.

They are not testifying to belief in God, much less enacting obedience to divine law. Their pledge of allegiance is rather to *the community and its traditions*. The relevant "faith" is often not faith in God but faith in Torah, in Israel, in the ultimate meaning to be secured from living in the framework defined at Sinai and passing on that framework to future generations. And the search for God—as I have learned from hundreds of conversations with Jews around the country—has often proved a source of great meaning as well, and has sometimes even led to faith.

"Would that they abandon me, but [continue to] observe my Torah," God says in a daring rabbinic homily.[4] The author of the Sinai covenant knew that faith without commandments cannot stand. But commandments, covenant, the communal life of Israel, are designed to take Jews higher.

It is crucial that Jews considering acceptance of the covenant on these terms understand that, according to the framework passed down to us from Sinai, no blind allegiance is required. That is certainly the case in our day, when all matters of communal policy are vigorously debated, and affiliation cannot be coerced in any case. This is a contract from which one can withdraw at any time. But in one sense that has *always* been true. Judaism has never been an all or nothing, take it or leave it, matter. Life according to the Torah cannot ever be objectified into a discrete "it" independent of the living Jews who carry on the conversation that Sinai initiated. Criticism, interpretation, diverse understanding are ever essential. The "Covenant Code" of chapters 20–23 of Exodus cannot be comprehended without reams of commentary. One must know, for example—and the Torah does not tell us—what exactly constitutes "labor" on the seventh day. How else could we punish it? One must know the details of every situation if justice is to be done and the good well served.

Hence the rabbis' conviction that Moses must have received an "Oral Law" along with the words that we have in the Torah, black on white. They exposited that oral law by applying age-old precepts to unprecedented conditions. We still do that—not only in books written by rabbis or scholars but in the interpretations implicit in individuals acts of mitzvah, every day. The meaning of the law is never fixed. We ourselves help to determine it, once we have stepped inside the framework of mitzvah. That is in my view the sense of the

Israelites' declaration "We will do and we will hear." One can only hear from the midst of the doing. What can be heard is a function of what Jews, partners to the covenant, have done.

Other Jews, likewise seizing hold of a possibility opened up by the Torah, approach the covenant initially or primarily "from God's side." This means, to a person such as myself, arriving at Sinai via experiences of gratitude or blessing, of challenge or of terror, experiences that confirm God's presence in the world and call upon us to live accordingly. For the rabbis, this aspect of the covenant was of course self-evident; God was simply there, sometimes more than they would have wished. For me, however, a professing Jew and professor of Judaism, engagement with God has been a nearly life-long and often frustrating pursuit. The sense of relation or proximity to God in my experience has been far from constant. God is in the world, as Jacob says, and often I do not know it. And then, all at once, I do. The recognition comes in boundary moments of birth and death, or perceptions of nature as a wondrous whole, or intimations of transcendence in history, or flashes of discernment that light up texts we read or actions we perform—moments that afterward refuse to be snuffed out by counter-experiences of meaninglessness or by rational analysis that explains them away.

The birth of my first child was such a moment. She emerged from the womb and I cried out instinctively, "Thank God." I had taken Lamaze classes, reviewed my high school biology, gained some understanding of the process of human reproduction—and still could not persuade myself that my wife and I alone had brought our daughter into being. The language of miracle at the instant of childbirth seems insufficient rather than sentimental; the only question is whether one can hold onto the experience later on: "abide," as Buber put it, "in the astonishment."

My friends, sitting around informally late at night, almost all report encounters with the Ultimate of this sort, and often even the avowed secularists among them are not loath to associate these experiences with God. I myself have known my share: like the day I stood before the Western Wall in Jerusalem, prayed sincerely for a prayer and the ability to pray it, and then saw fluttering toward me in the breeze a Hebrew page torn out of a book. I recognized it at once: "Ashrei," Psalm 146, a prayer I knew by heart. The way to good faith, I believe, lies in not making more of such experiences than integrity allows, not smothering the doubts, but also in not making *less* of them than integrity allows, not permitting the doubts entirely to hold sway. The trick, as Abraham Heschel wrote, is to open ourselves to what he called the awe and wonder of the "ineffable"— and then to "tell it to our minds."[5]

This is not easy, never has been easy. Many people in our generation are kept from faith by problems which inevitably arise in connection with relation to God and God's commandments. Two such issues are immediately evident in my reading of Exodus 19. I note them here because for contemporary American Jews such as myself they cannot be avoided.

The first is *authority*: the Torah's presumption that human beings *need laws* in order to do the good, and need them to *be revealed* to us by God. Revelation, for Torah, *is* law. How should we understand these assumptions? Can we assent to them? Why isn't reason, operating through philosophers and lawgivers, sufficient to provide us with all the laws we need to do the good and all the knowledge we need to discern it?

Faith itself is the second issue. Belief in the God of Nature is one thing, but who is the God at Sinai, who speaks to prophets and battles kings? What would it mean to believe that God actually "descended" on the mountain? The anthropomorphic imagery is the least of our worries. The Torah knows God has no body. What matters is the claim that God could and did "reveal" something to human beings, i.e., enter time and space, speak to people like you and me, get involved in human history. What can Jews today "see" in this revelation? What should they "hear"?

I will take up each of these matters in turn.

Reason, Tradition, and Experience

The Torah's verdict on the venerable questions of whether reason can show us the good, and whether once we know the good we can be trusted to do it, is well supported in the literature of social and political theory—but likely to displease many late-twentieth-century Americans. For the text presumes that unaided reason will not achieve the knowledge of the good that we require. Nor will knowing what the good is necessarily cause us to choose to do it. Trust in either the adequacy of mind or the pure goodness of heart should, in the Torah's view, be adjudged mere sentimentality.

This does not mean that human goodness is impossible or that human reason is useless. Either of those assumptions would preclude human transformation of the world and so render Torah utterly pointless. Exodus is rather determined to have reason recognize and work on its own shortcomings. God's plan is apparently to take human nature as it is and ever shall be—capable but fallible in judgment; capable of doing good as well as evil—and nonetheless to raise the species, starting with Israel, to as much holiness as is humanly possible. God's creatures shall become God's partners in carrying Creation to fulfillment.

There is patent *chutzpa* in this perspective. As Nietzsche pointed out perceptively, life always involves the shedding of blood. The whole of nature operates through violence, "and yet old Moses said, 'Thou shalt not kill.'"[6] There is also a degree of pessimism in the Torah's outlook, which—depending on one's point of view—will either count as sober realism or unabated cynicism. Moses assumes that the effort to rise above instinct, though always worth attempting, can never entirely succeed. The Ten Commandments are not easily obeyed. Murder, theft, and adultery remain commonplace. Coveting (if understood to be a matter of intention rather than of action) is by definition coterminous with desire, and thus irrepressible. The command to honor parents is made necessary in every generation—and made difficult—by profound and eternal ambivalence. Idolatry too seems a deep-rooted inclination, not easily exterminated. God thus has to contend for loyalty that, given a different creation (and different intentions of the Creator), might well have come more easily. The Torah knows all this and yet seems to presume that the struggle is not in vain. One can, to a degree at least, obey the commandments. Else why command them? Human beings can reason well about the good—or it is folly to entrust the world, and the Torah, to our keeping.

Each of us has to take a stand on these matters. They are far from abstract. Are we going to trust our neighbors or aren't we? Are our children destined to repeat our own mistakes or are they not? Can the world be improved or can't it? Shall we resign ourselves to a social order ruled by violence? Do we believe in love? The Torah's approach, echoed in the modern period most closely by Rousseau, I think, is to "take men as they are, and laws as they might be." It avoids utopian views of human goodness on the one hand and Augustinian notions of original sin on the other, and still hopes for more than a "war of all against all," i.e., violence constrained only by the fear of greater violence. There can be, the Torah insists, a "legitimate and sure principle of government" (Rousseau's phrase in *The Social Contract*) which can guide us toward the right: not because the "general will" never errs (Rousseau's mistake, demonstrably false since the Golden Calf), but because God had added revelation (and so the tradition based upon it) to the resources available.

We are not on our own. *Reason* and *experience* can call in Torah to assist, thanks to the *tradition* which enables it to reach us, the tradition itself deriving from all three—reason, experience, and revelation, prior tradition—working together.

By this point in my life, the Torah's cautious opinion of human merit and human reason has come to seem compelling. The need for law as a directive to individual goodness is to my mind utterly self-evident. I watch my children grow, dispensing both cruelty and kindness to one another daily. They in turn watch me hurt those I love most, often failing to do the good I know I should be doing. I've grown well acquainted with my personal temptations and therefore cherish rules which force me to do what otherwise, left to my own devices, I might not. Transgressive and self-destructive drives are ever-present. Who can deny them after what Freud and all the rest of our awful century have taught? Restraint, if moderate and wise, has become as precious to me as freedom. This is basic stuff in middle age, affecting the way we live and teach and parent. It also seems basic stuff to contemporary social theory, no longer enamored of unbridled human potential and far from convinced that human beings, left to their own devices, can be counted on for virtue.

I have also come to agree with the Torah's view of reason, which now seems to me a precious but extremely frail instrument: for most purposes it's all we have to go on, yet woefully inadequate to our needs, individual or collective. I am as respectful as anyone of reason's achievements in the sciences, grateful for the technology it has made possible, indebted to the degree of mastery over nature's secrets that is obviously and justly a source for wonder. I have found no better tool for puzzling through the ethical dilemmas which all of us confront daily, and believe in no better instrument for organizing the institutions of the world.

Yet we are so often in the dark regarding the rights and wrongs that loom before us. Philosophers argue no less now than ever over all the fundamental questions. Smarter people seem to me no more virtuous than other people. The evil uses to which reason has been put, and reason's own apparent willingness to turn its awesome energies to accomplishing obvious evil, are more apparent after the Holocaust than ever before. Freud has destroyed the notion that reason operates independently of our basest drives, let alone exercises sovereignty over them. Marx and Hegel have long since challenged reason's independence of social forces. More than "reason alone" seems required, despite what Kant thought, to get us to the Good. Science constantly turns up more mysteries than it has the wherewithal to penetrate, while love continues to present mysteries to all of us, which—if we are wise—we do not attempt merely to think through.

There is a prima facie case in favor of religious traditions, which—very much like love—have proven useful over the centuries (though far from perfect, God knows) in the attempt by many individuals and cultures to discern and teach the true and the good. The case for Judaism seems particularly strong, and not only because I know it best. The Torah compels me as well because it has never argued for blind obedience, or for the dismissal of reason in favor of instinct or passion, or for submission to "the voice within." Such appeals quite frankly scare me to death, as they scared the rabbis long ago. The Torah's imperatives are not simply written black on white but must be pondered. For Jews it is axiomatic that fundamentalism is anathema. One never reads the text without interpretation, i.e., tradition. Children study Torah with Rashi for that reason. And Rashi, like every other contributor to the tradition, drew on reason and experience to figure out what God, via Torah, was commanding him.

That is why the Torah's claims concerning Sinai deserve a hearing before twentieth-century minds despite the fact that we have all been well trained (and with good reason) to be skeptical of all claims to ultimate authority and are all suspicious, for still better reasons, of

Exodus: History, Faith, and Covenant

religious authority. That hearing can and does take place, I think, because God's announced purposes at Sinai involved "heart and soul and might." The human faculties, the Creator knew, cannot easily be disentangled. "Mind" cannot be entirely separated from "heart," as if reason and emotion were unconnected. The Torah in fact refers to both in a single word: *lev*. Nor can we keep what we learn from revelation, via tradition, in a separate "pocket" isolated from all we learn from other sources. Moses presumably learned a lot at Pharaoh's court and brought it with him to Sinai. He consults his father-in-law once he gets there about the best way to administer justice. The Israelites drew then and later on the high culture of Babylonia, as we learn from Shakespeare and Cezanne, Plato and George Eliot. Torah demands no monopoly on mind and claims no copyright on the soul.

Nor, as I have argued more than once, can one simply take in "Revelation" uncritically, as if God's word were "out there" for the asking to assuage perplexity and banish doubt if only one obeys. The Torah was well aware of atrocities committed in gods' names by people convinced they had acted upon the authority of revelation. It models the proper response to authority in Abraham's interrogation of God when he hears of the plan to destroy Sodom and Gomorrah. "Shall not the judge of all earth do justly?" The Torah does not allow us for even a moment to dispense with reason or experience.

It rather demands—as in Exodus 20–23—the rational application of legal precedents and principles. The rabbis modeled this for us with enthusiasm. Could the Torah really sentence the person who gouges an eye to have his or her own eye gouged? What, they reasoned, would be the point? "Eye for eye, tooth for tooth" could not be taken literally. The text requires expositors like the rabbis. In our day too it does not demand obedience but interpretation—which can occur only inside communities of people committed to conducting this process and living with one another according to its outcome.

And the community in turn depends upon this process for its survival. How will Judaism ever be compelling in America unless, like Israel, it is seen to matter in the concrete details of social life? How will the Jewish community survive the situation of voluntarism as a tiny minority of the population unless it is bound together by commitments more lasting than individual decisions to participate in individual events in a given year or month or week? The authority and commandment initiated at Sinai need us if they are to survive in the world *and vice versa.*

The same requirement of interpretation holds true, must ever hold true, when it comes to matters of *faith.* In the encounter with the presence of God, neither reason nor experience is silenced. We are rather meant to hold up what we have been taught by Torah to the facts of the world as we know them—and vice versa. Mind as well as emotion, experience as much as a tradition of commentary, must be consulted as we work to find our way to faith. Just as the Torah refuses to choose between belief in innate human goodness and belief in inveterate human evil, so we need not and cannot choose between faith and reason, or faith and science. We don't leave any crucial faculty behind us as we approach Sinai—certainly not our minds.

Heschel, in an effort to protect faith from rational attack—to carve out space, as it were, in which faith could rest secure from the demand for rational "proof"—put forward the notion that religion belongs to a different domain than reason. "Soul and reason are not the same. . . . The search of reason ends at the shore of the known; on the immense expanse beyond it only the ineffable can glide. Citizens of two realms, we all must sustain a dual allegiance. . . ."[7] In its weaker form, the claim seems correct, in fact a truism. Reason alone is insufficient to comprehend divinity. Language cannot capture the ineffable. In any stronger form, however—the argument that reason must be set aside to find God, that it has no role in the search—the claim seems to me (based on my own use of reason, tradition, and experience) to be mistaken, even dangerous. Heschel himself never endorsed it. How could he? The Torah explicitly demands the engagement of "heart and soul and might"; we bring all we have to the question of faith, and bring it as the individuals we are—heirs to our families, members in a particular people, witnesses to a certain history, participants in one or more particular languages, cultures, traditions. Heschel not only advocated such service, but embodied it.

This understanding of the road to faith is as old as the rabbinic tradition in Judaism; no Jewish thinker has articulated it as clearly as Moses Maimonides (1135–1204), who—before he could engage a difficult matter such as the nature of God—found it necessary to absorb the best that Greek and Arabic science and philosophy had to teach. Before he pronounced on matters still more unknowable in his view, such as what awaits us after death, Maimonides had to disabuse his readers of the notion that the Torah had answered all such questions forthrightly. Some Jews, Maimonides wrote, expected to be rewarded corporeally for their good deeds, whether in this world or in the world to come: a grave error, he advised, and an expectation worthy only of children. Adults should not need the promise of treats in order to do what is right, and should know they will not receive them. Other Jews, Maimonides continued, correctly ridiculed the idea of corporeal reward—but mistakenly believed it to be the normative teaching of Judaism and took that as an excuse for turning their backs on Torah, perhaps even on God, altogether.

There was, however, a third group of interpreters, "to whom the greatness of our sages is clear. They recognize . . . that the words of the sages contain both an obvious and a hidden meaning." The Bible necessarily spoke in the "language of human beings" and not always in that of the wisest human beings. It used metaphor and parable. The text was not self-explanatory. One had to interpret it. Philosophy, far from superfluous, held the key.[8] Other Jewish philosophers— Yehudah Halevi, for example—were less sanguine than Maimonides about the virtues of philosophy and stressed instead the need for wisdom that accrues through pious obedience to God's commandments. But they too, albeit in different balance, embraced both "reason" and "revelation."

All knew the contrast in the rabbinic tradition between Rabbi Akiba and his colleague Rabbi Ishmael over the meaning of the command to "love the Lord your God." Akiba, the "mystic," took the verse literally: demanding a personal relationship to a God unseen. Ishmael, a thousand years before the medieval philosophers, and two thousand before the moderns, said that the command could mean only one thing: to "love your neighbor as yourself."[9]

Allies as powerful as these, precedents as venerable as these, are indispensable to a contemporary Jew such as myself, who is convinced that God remains concealed in cloud and fire—as against Jewish partisans of the view that their view and only their view is "Torah-true," and skeptics who believe that the fire and cloud conceal nothing at all, that all claims of divinity are nonsense. I am also grateful for contemporary non-Jewish allies who list religion, as the philosopher Charles Taylor does, among the "sources of the self" and work to chart the complex inter-relationship among reason, tradition, and experience; or who, like Alasdair MacIntyre, urge that ethics be reconnected to the guidance of religious traditions and the restraints of communal obligation.[10] They and other philosophers have recently been arguing for a renewed partnership between forces that since the Enlightenment have been held in many quarters to be enemies. Jewish thinkers from Hermann Cohen and Franz Rosenzweig at the start of the twentieth century to Emil Fackenheim and Emmanuel Levinas at its conclusion have been doing the same. Even militantly secular partisans of reason no longer hold that we draw upon a pure faculty of thought when making ethical decisions or pondering the Ultimate. It is common knowledge that our thought is "situated." We remain within *traditions* of how to think and what thinking means. The Torah—ever open to reflection and solicitous of interpretation—certainly qualifies as one which contemporary Jews should be consulting.

When it comes to revelation, one can only ask questions of this text. What did the Israelites hear at Sinai? Would a tape recorder turned on at the right moment have captured a human-like voice intoning the Ten Commandments: probably a deep voice, like in the movie? Or would it have recorded only the sounds of thunder and shofar? Did Moses hear only what everyone else heard? Or did he receive an expanded revelation—via conscience, perhaps, or a prelinguistic intuition of the divine will, or a perception born of surpassingly great love for God and Israel as one? Definitive answers are precluded by the Torah itself; as Heschel pointed out, belief in "Torah from Heaven" is the foundation of Jewish law, but that doctrine is not *halakha* but *aggada*. Jews can and must disagree over how revelation transpired, and all the more over what it entails.

At times I myself follow Heschel and Buber in picturing God in personal terms: in affirming, that is, that the ability to relate "person to person" is among God's infinite attributes. The philosophical problems with this, I know, are immense. Yet personal experience seems to demand it. Heschel captured his own experience beautifully (or so I infer) in *Man Is Not Alone*.

> A moment comes like a thunderbolt, in which a flash of the undisclosed rends our deep apathy asunder. It is full of overpowering bril-

liance. . . . The ineffable has shuddered itself into the soul. It has entered our consciousness like a ray of light passing into a lake. . . . A cry, wrested from our very core, fills the world around us, as if a mountain were suddenly about to place itself in front of us. It is one word: GOD: Not an emotion, a stir within us, but a power, a marvel beyond us, tearing the world apart.[11]

Buber, not much less eloquently, wrote that we glimpse the Eternal Thou through every I-Thou relation of wholeness and real presence. Sinai was to him a stammering account of actual Israelite experience: "the verbal trace of a natural event, i.e., of an event which took place in the world of the senses common to all men, and fitted into connections which the senses can perceive." It was experienced as revelation communicated to each of them, "its witness, to his constitution, to his life, to his sense of duty." God had spoken to Buber himself, had encountered him, right here in the twentieth century. Why should one not believe that the same had happened to ancient Israelites at Sinai?[12]

Without the confidence of either thinker, I would simply report the experiences that transpired at my children's births and other moments of special urgency and cite the manifold blessings which have reached me and for which I am driven to thank the Creator of all life. I confess my indebtedness to this God readily, give voice to my gratitude for being. I have no trouble waking in the morning and, following the traditional Jewish rite, thanking God for breath as I yawn deeply, or for the "orifices without which we could not survive for a single instant." Blessing God for making me upright comes naturally as I stretch. Accepting the command to clothe the naked, as I find clothes in the closet, seems not merely abstract moral duty but the directive of a Creator close at hand.

And what of revelation? Chapter 19 of Exodus well reports my own experience of seeking after God. Ups and downs. Sightings followed by concealments. You are there and then you are not. God is there, or here, and then is not. Here and there become confused. The top of the mountain can be the deepest recesses within one's heart and soul. A chair in the garden at twilight can be all the bounded space that God needs for a descent. Reason, tradition, experience—and faith—all join in this testimony of divine presence in the world.

At other moments I prefer (and am driven) to picture God in

impersonal terms: a force (or set of forces) of Nature, as Spinoza and Mordecai Kaplan insisted. Philosophy is somewhat more amenable to this idea (though it too comes in for its share of criticism). As a colleague of mine put it, summarizing the view of the philosopher Leo Strauss, "The strictly knowable God will [always] be impersonal and the distinctly personal God will be mysterious." Philosophy, reason, will always prefer the former option—but experience also testifies on its behalf. We look at the stars, marvel at a sunset, try to take in the scientists' talk of aeons and galaxies and infinity. We *sense* that we are part of it all, can even *think* our way to that conclusion, and perhaps also arrive at the thought that reason belongs to God's creation as much as the stars, and brings word to conscience of moral laws no less eternal than the rocks and no less the gift of the Creator.

Were the Jewish mystics bearing witness to a personal or an impersonal conception of God with their infinite images of the Ultimate, their grand metaphor of ten spheres into which divinity emanates and through which it fills the cosmos, and their notion that behind the point of origin, concealed in ultimate Ultimacy, lies the "En Sof" or No End—also called "Ayin" or No Thing? Is this the God who is referred to by a four-letter, unpronounceable personal name in the Torah, the one who intervened in Egypt to save the Israelites and is identified with the divine attribute of mercy, the God who called Moses up the mountain in Exodus 19:3? Or is it *Elohim*, the God of Nature and Judgment, possessed of no personal name—who, according to Exodus 20:1, was the source of the Ten Commandments, laws as eternal as the growth of spring? "They have imagined you, but not as you are," says the kabbalistic Hymn of Glory. "They have pictured you in a thousand metaphors. But you are one in all imaginings."

I cannot decide once and for all among these and other possibilities. At some moments I am drawn more to one mode of relation to God, and at other moments to others. God's presence alternately seems manifest in a ritual, a text, an act of kindness—or is nowhere to be found. Doubt sometimes gives way to real despair, and at other times is countered by a kind of gut faith that the Protestant theologian Paul Tillich well captured in the phrase "the courage to be." There are days when I follow the instruction given the prophet Elijah, who stood at Sinai many generations after Moses, but was told to look for God in the "still small voice" rather than in the thunder or the whirlwind. On other days the still small voice is of no avail. I turn up the volume in my head to full power, letting the varied sounds of tradition and experience resonate at all the volume I can stand. And at still other moments I strain to hear God in complete silence and seek there too in vain. The quiet proves no more helpful than full volume. The Ultimate is Ayin, Nowhere.

The Torah seems to understand this predicament and to prepare for it. So did the rabbis and the mystics. In synagogue, following the guidance of the Hymn of Glory recited in the course of Sabbath services, I always come at the words in the prayerbook wearing multiple headsets that supply images as I go and power the mute words on the page into life. How else sing praises to "You, for whom my soul yearns"? How else guard, and attend to, the Mystery? The cacophony is frustrating only when I feel a need to resolve matters: when the burden of ignorance (as in the face of suffering) has come to seem unbearable. Usually, however, I treasure the plurality of voices emanating from Sinai, as I welcome the revival of serious God-talk which has taken place in recent years among American Jews. Feminists, naturalists, mystics, rational theists, and learned atheists are once more sharing the benefit of their thought and experience more widely. We have even begun to bring Torah into dialogue with the highest achievements of modern culture: science, art, and philosophy; the professions; new wisdom about the self.

Now as ever there is no purpose in seeking consensus in this endeavor, and no possibility of achieving it. The point remains the conversation. God-talk too is part of covenant, after all: a need of the spirit which Jews, whether focused single-mindedly on communal observance or surrendering to the secularism of the times, have too long and too often ignored. Judaism—and not only we ourselves—has been the poorer for it.

Knowing God, Doing Good

It seems fair to say that even with the best of intentions and the most resolute determination to overcome the challenges of modernity, faith will remain fragmentary for most contemporary Jews: a remnant of the involvement with God which, our sources indicate, once was. Faith and covenant both will likely continue to provide less meaning than we desire, even if more than we might have expected.

I at least cannot seem to grasp hold for very long of any of the certainties for which I yearn. More and more, therefore, I have found the account of Moses' next solo ascent up Sinai—in the aftermath of the golden calf—an invaluable source of consolation.

The Torah once more begins (in chapter 32) where we are, down below. The mountain is again covered in cloud. The only person who can even claim to have intimate knowledge of God is not with us. He has departed, and after forty days we have become unsure that he will return. We are waiting anxiously. I think I remain within the text's intent when I read it as a depiction of the human situation as the Torah understands it. We humans are bounded by the four walls of our existence. We cannot escape our bodies, to be or join another. We cannot step outside our minds to look out of this life from another perspective, another culture. We cannot escape the limits of time or defy our mortality. And as a result of these three, there is wall number four: we cannot know God, who is bounded by neither body nor mind nor time.

Hence the immense human longing for the God whom we glimpse in moments of history such as the Exodus, the God of whom we know something from nature and whom we encounter on rare occasions of blessing in our lives. Occasionally, the longing becomes unbearable, and when it does we can either pull away and despair of knowing God altogether, or, as the Israelites do here, try to break through the four walls and create our own image of God—and then worship it: "The people offered up burnt offerings [to the golden calf] and brought sacrifices of well-being; they sat down to eat and drink, and then rose to dance."

The rabbis, I think, were justified in bending over backward in midrash to excuse the fashioning of the calf. They well understood the psychological, indeed spiritual, necessity involved. For they had themselves experienced the pain of longing for God, perhaps exacerbated by Judaism's prohibition on creating images of God. They too were surrounded by idolaters who had gods ready-made, up close. No Jew was or is exempt from this predicament, including Moses. When the scene shifts to the top of the mountain, we find him saying to God: "Look, you tell me, 'take up this people,' but you have not let me know whom you will send with me, and you have said, 'I have known you by name,' and also that I have found favor in your eyes, but now please if I have found favor in your eyes, let me know your ways, and let me know you, so that I can find favor in your eyes [in the future]" (33:12–13). In other words: tell me what I desperately need to know! Tell me what I'm doing right! "Show me your glory." Let me know what lies beyond history, beyond mind, beyond all knowledge and all beyonds.

To which God responds, in a theological high point of the Torah, "I will cause all my goodness to pass upon [or: before] your face, and I will call out the name of the Lord before you [literally: to your face]. And I will be gracious to whom I will be gracious, and will show compassion to whom I will show compassion. But," He said, "You cannot see my face, because no man may see my face and live." Moses will see only God's "back"—the place, perhaps, where God has been: God's handiwork, or God's revelation, or perhaps the miraculous saving events witnessed by our ancestors. Even in chapter 24, where Moses and others ascend the mountain and are said to "see" the God of Israel—"and under His feet there was the likeness of a pavement of sapphire, like the very sky for purity"—even there one does not really see God but sees *below* God, as it were, the metaphorical character of the word "feet" underlined by the very next sentence: "Yet He did not raise His hand against the leaders of the Israelites; they beheld God, and they ate and drank."

Again we are forced to ask: just what did those Israelites see? Moses has seen more of God than anyone, and even he cannot see God's face. For the face is the distinguishing organ of the person, and to read the face, to see into the eyes, is to know a great deal of the person. Such knowledge of God is beyond mortal capacity. The text constitutes a reflection—crucial, profound, and full of pathos—on the human need and desire to know what cannot be known. A story of the golden calf necessarily had to follow the account of revelation—revealing the limits of the learning which Sinai makes possible. Religious language cannot but personify God's bodily features, all the while focusing attention—in part through the prohibition on visual imagery—on its own tragically metaphorical character. We stand at a great remove. As if the subject of its meditation were not clear enough, this section of Exodus teems with ordinary Hebrew expressions that build the word "face" into simple words like "before" and "upon."

Chapter 34 concludes with the remarkable story that Moses himself had to cover his face when returning from God's presence, for it shown with bright light. Moses' own example as seen by the Israelites points to that which cannot be seen or expressed. The text in which we read about both concealments does the same. We need to look away, to the place where God has been. We have to seek through indirection. God's own hand, as it were, shields us from what we cannot behold in this life. "Revelation" is required if we are to believe in God and so obey the laws of Moses—and so, therefore, is concealment. Divine energy, the text seems to say, would otherwise blind us and strike us dead. How can we look on God if we cannot see at all in Jerusalem's noonday sun without squinting?

The divine self-description in chapter 34—the minimum we can and must know of God, according to this account, and very close to the maximum which we can know—reduces to two attributes: law and mercy. Neither is a surprise, given all that has come before. Reason, tradition, and experience could have supplied them. A God as truly concerned with humanity as this God is, a partner to covenant, must be concerned with the details of sacred order in which human beings pass their days. God must care passionately about justice. "Le bon Dieu est dans les details." The Good Lord is in the details, for that is where we are, and if God cares about us, God will be there too. God must be near at hand, and so (because God is God and we are not) God must judge us. The accounting transpires over many generations because—as we learn from Genesis—the meaning of a life often cannot be discerned within its own span alone. It can be read only in the lives of children or grandchildren. History all too often visits the sins of parents on children and grandchildren.

And if we or our descendants are to survive divine judgment, God must also be merciful. Whatever that means in the ultimate scheme of things that remains beyond our knowing, for us God's mercy means at the very least that God's kindness exceeds God's punishment: that God loves life and will act to further it. Otherwise we could not abide God's presence among us, nor God ours. The world could not proceed. This much the text thinks it does know. Reason and experience here concur.

Not the least part of the mercy or loving kindness that God bestows (via human consciousnesses like that of Moses) are the regulations of tabernacle and priesthood that comprise the final third of the Book of Exodus. In the absence of God's direct presence and guidance, in the necessary distance which God must keep if we are to live, in the eternal pondering of eternal verities without satisfactory resolution, lies the origin of *religion*. It is a divine invention (meaning: a human invention authorized and perhaps inspired by experience of God) intended to preserve faith in spite of the evils that human hearts will at times desire and human eyes will see, and in spite of the saving blindness which keeps us from ever really knowing God. Doubt is built into the enterprise of faith. Events like the construction of the golden calf will always follow on experiences of revelation, even when the latter are as momentous as those at Sinai and are accompanied by amazing displays of lightning and thunder. For how can we ever be sure of God's voice behind the thunders—let alone be sure that we are hearing it correctly? Salvation at the Red Sea is necessarily and immediately followed by concern over where the next meal, the next drink of water, will come from. Human beings cannot live on bread alone, to be sure—but neither can they live exclusively on "what comes forth out of the mouth of the Lord." The holy must be available every day, morning and evening, informing what we eat and how we love.

That is particularly true when, as in our generation, the Lord seems distant, and God's presence in the details is so very much in doubt. All the more need, then, for interpretations of Sinai that render the word of God in Torah adequate to basic—and ever-changing—human needs; all the more need, especially, for *religion,* which can step into the breach of disbelief with rituals that continue to provide meaning and sustain covenant even when a surer faith is lacking. Ritual helps us sustain the possibility of repairing the world, which we cannot fully understand or save. Prophecy requires priests. Covenant requires sanctuary. Exodus requires Leviticus.

Before turning to the Torah's third book, I will conclude with one final rabbinic reflection (found in the Babylonian Talmud, Tractate Baba Batra 10a) in which the issues of Exodus—and this chapter—are not only addressed but formulated in a way that to my mind says all that can be said on the subject of getting past history to faith and covenant—and not a syllable more.

"It has been taught: Rabbi Meir used to say: The critic [of Judaism] may bring against you the argument, If your God loves the poor, why does He not support them?" The question is a very good one. It represents a critique of Judaism, and not of paganism, because the chaos we see in the world would, if there were many competing gods, be perfectly understandable. God would fight god, now and forevermore. But if there is one God, concerned with the world, and that God is good, why then so much suffering? The question strikes at the very heart of all that Judaism teaches.

"If so, answer him, So that through them we may be saved from the punishment of Gehinnom [hell]." A terrible answer. God allows the poor to suffer so that we can perform acts of charity and thereby get to Heaven?! This can't be serious. And it isn't; the passage only begins here, after all. More is needed, and is forthcoming.

"This question was actually put by Turnus Rufus to Rabbi Akiba: If your God loves the poor, why does He not support them? He replied, So that we may be saved through them from the punishment of Gehinnom." This contextualizes the debate. Philosophy becomes story. Torah, as always, must be faced in the midst of history. Akiba was Meir's teacher, and, as the quintessential rabbinic sage, the teacher of all of us. Turnus Rufus was, by talmudic tradition, the Roman general who put Akiba to death for the crime of teaching Torah when the Romans had forbidden it. The argument is no longer academic. It is a matter of life and death. Now we are prepared to engage it properly.

"On the contrary," said Turnus Rufus, "it is this which condemns you to Gehinnom. I will illustrate by a parable. Suppose an earthly king was angry with his servant and put him in prison and ordered that he should be given no food or drink, and a man went and gave him food and drink. If the king heard, would he not be angry with him? And you are called servants, as it is written [Leviticus 25: 25] 'For unto me the children of Israel are servants.'"

We must carefully follow Turnus Rufus's move here, expressed in the choice of proof text, for the entire passage turns on it. According to the Roman's argument, Jews (who feed the poor, rather than letting them starve) should be compared to the man who gives food and drink to the imprisoned servant of the king. If God rules the world, so the logic goes, surely God intends the poor to be poor. Then we should leave them in that state! But Turnus Rufus gives his intention away (and that of the narrative) by comparing Israel, not to the man who brings the servant food, but to the servant who has been put in prison. A dialogue about charity has become a debate about politics. If the poor are meant to be poor, the losers of history are meant to be losers—and the winners are meant to win. If you believe in a God who controls the flow of history, Turnus Rufus says to Akiba, then I am meant to be putting you to death! Might is the demonstration of right! Appeal to the facts is always the strongest argument one can make.

But Akiba, who accepts the premise of divine involvement in history in a way most of us refuse to do regarding the Holocaust, is loyal to a higher authority than mere reality—and he at once invokes it. "I will illustrate by another parable. Suppose an earthly king was angry with his *son,* and put him in prison and ordered that no food or drink should be given to him, and someone went and gave him food and drink. If the king heard of it, would he not send him a present? And we are called sons, as it is written, 'Sons [or: children] are you to the Lord your God'" (Deuteronomy 14:1).

No matter what a parent may say in the heat of anger, there are natural bonds which outlast and supersede ephemeral words. Jews, and human beings generally, are God's children, and we are all commanded—by nature and by Torah—to treat them as such. Akiba cites no text to demonstrate this obligation of parents to children. It is to him self-evident. One need not be a Jew, need not have Torah, to understand and subscribe to it.

Turnus Rufus must therefore reply with a countervailing text that challenges our status as God's children. "You are called both sons and servants. When you carry out the desires of God you are called sons, and when you do not carry out the desires of God you are called servants. At the present time you are not carrying out the desires of God." For if you were, he reasons, you would be receiving reward, as you yourself said, not punishment at my hands.

Akiba rejects this line of argument. "Scripture says, 'Is it not [our obligation] to deal your bread to the hungry and bring the poor that are cast out into your house?' (Isaiah 58:7). When must we do this? Now!" In other words: always. Akiba knows full well what God demands. He learned it from reason and Torah, obligations which in this case have been forcefully reiterated by Isaiah. He does not and never will understand why, obeying God, we all too often suffer while those who flout God's will seem to prosper. Reason cannot find its way around that eternal conundrum. But neither, as this passage teaches, can "revelation." Akiba, like Moses, has no answer to the perplexities that most concern him. He cannot see God's face and live. In fact, because of his teaching the text that contains that lesson, he is about to be killed. The narrative, like Exodus, offers no philosophical answer, but only reiterates the divine/moral demand in the face of the eternal human questions.

The demand, unlike the answer, is clear. Feed the poor, lest idolatry and immorality triumph, thereby denying ultimate meaning to both individual life and human history as a whole. Earth in that case would become hell—a place where losers are left to lose and the poor are left to suffer in their poverty. We cannot prevent this through full understanding of history's course. But we can work against it. Feed the poor!

That is perhaps the greatest comfort which the Torah holds out to us in our ignorance of the Ultimate, an ignorance which in our generation—enhanced by scientific discovery—perhaps seems larger and more profound than ever. We don't have to understand God, the rabbis aver: wrestling is all the possibility we have. We cannot comprehend the course of history in the best of times, and certainly not in the worst, but only face up to it, not stand aside. What we have to do, and fortunately can do, is act to repair the world that we have inherited, in the framework of a people dedicated to this purpose and a Torah designed to help us accomplish it. The covenants of fate and destiny have made this possible. They set a task which is worthy of a thousand lifetimes. It is certainly worthy of the one which each of us has received, perhaps with that very purpose in mind.

3

⚜

Leviticus

RITUAL AND COMMUNITY

The Book of Leviticus is not terribly popular among American Jews of my acquaintance. Take on the task of assigning members of a prayer or study group to lead discussions on upcoming portions of the Torah, and you will have no difficulty finding volunteers for most sections of Genesis or Exodus. Turn the pages of the calendar to the winter months, however, arrive at the blood and gore of sacrifice and the details upon details of purity and pollution, and you will find that interest in the weekly portion has withered. Leviticus seems so repetitive, so anachronistic. It strikes us as a primer for priests (hence the title of the book), a lecture intended for others on which we can at best eavesdrop. Indeed, the book is in many cases offensive to contemporary convictions and sensibilities. One wants simply to get through it, to escape the confining precincts of the tabernacle for the openness of wilderness: the gripping stories in the Book of Numbers. I too once felt this way.

Only recently have I come to see what I for so long missed in Leviticus, and to understand why I missed it. The first reason is that I was looking off to the distance, as it were, attempting to keep my eye on higher things like faith and covenant—Exodus concerns—when the interest of this book lies up close, in the foreground. It is a teaching about the everyday, *our* everyday included. Leviticus aims to heighten and sanctify ordinary experience. It wants us to focus on the possibilities for love and good stored up in daily life, and tries to accomplish this through a vision of *community* that is symbolized, and prepared for, in *ritual*. Far from being irrelevant to contemporary experience, then, Leviticus concentrates on precisely the two elements which many American Jews find most appealing in Jewish tradition, and which are arguably most crucial to the revitalization of American Jewish life.

The second barrier to appreciation of the gifts stored up in the book is the medium in which its message is couched. Leviticus envisions sacred order by means of a symbolic language that is opaque and at times disturbing to modern sensibilities. Its most salient term of art, front and center from the very first page, is sacrifice. The images of animal slaughter are both plentiful and graphic. More problematic still, I think, the book seeks at every point to build and maintain community through rules and regulations governing purity and pollution—and these too seem arcane or objectionable. The connection between exalted states of holiness and the minutiae of bodily intakes and excretions tends to escape us. As a result, Leviticus's demand that we pay attention to the details of everyday existence arouses boredom or displeasure far more than interest or excitement. It cannot command most Jews' attention anymore, let alone their behavior. The gap separating them from tradition seems in this case particularly immense. Small wonder that even many committed Jews do not make the effort to overcome it.

It is our loss, I think. Leviticus is the best framework I know for discussing Jewish ritual and community—two primary focuses of its concern, and mine—and one of the most profound articulations I have encountered in this or any tradition of the possibility, in and through ritual and community, of sanctifying everyday life. My aim is to add further impetus to the reinvigoration of ritual and community already underway among American Jews by drawing on Leviticus's effort to engage its readers with meaning so rich and deep, and a vision of community so palpable, that they will wish to be part of them.

My sketch of the community possible in contemporary America will of course not endorse many of Leviticus's prescriptions, just as the varieties of ritual observance today will necessarily depart significantly from Leviticus as well as from the prior departures of the mystics, philosophers, and rabbis. Both will also fall far short of the sacred order which the book seeks to place at the disposal of its readers' imaginations. Leviticus pictures an Israelite camp splendidly isolated in the wilderness, or a promised land set apart by God's love and God's protection. The rabbis too pictured a holy nation living apart from the nations of the world. Neither vision suits our situation. Jewish communities in contemporary America, I shall argue, must by contrast be *voluntary, multiple,* and *pluralist*—as befits life in a society and culture of which Jews are thoroughly a part, and which has become thoroughly a part of American Jews. Leviticus clearly has something very different in mind.

Our continuity with its vision, however, can nonetheless be substantial. It lies, first, in the strategy of engaging Jewish commitment with a combination of meaning and community so powerful that Jews return for more. This is already the case with hundreds of thousands of Jews in this country. The combination could be provided to millions of others. Every piece of evidence we have about American Jewry confirms that all of the programs and institutions most successful in fostering strong Jewish identity—camps, Israel trips, day schools, synagogues that are congregations in more than name only—are frameworks in which palpable meaning and community are held out to Jews, and held out to them together. Moreover, in keeping with Leviticus's emphasis upon detail, I will try not only to give a sense of what Jewish community should *ideally* look like in our day but also offer some *concrete* steps by which it can be achieved and sustained. One of the things I have most come to respect in Leviticus—part and parcel of the book's refusal to entertain—is its insistence that we attend to the "nitty-gritty" that comprises daily life rather than allowing escape either into trivial pursuits or to grander matters like Revelation and Creation. God is very much "in the details" for Leviticus, because that is where we are.

American Jewry has proven itself to be very talented at rising to mythic occasion such as the Six-Day War or Operation Exodus, the rescue of Soviet Jews. It has been far less successful at offering the sort of meaning comprehensive enough to sanctify even daily routine. We have yet to find a way, in this or any other modern diaspora, of bringing Jewish meaning to the places where Jews stand, not once or twice a year but all the time. That is the task confronting us, however, and it has been accepted as such by the movement for "Jewish continuity" that has taken hold in recent years. Leviticus, I think, not only holds out the hope that we *can* do this in America but points the way to its achievement. In this chapter we shall follow the progression which it sets forth, moving from ritual to community to love.

The Art of Ritual

We can most usefully begin our journey into the symbolic world of Leviticus by noting—in the book's opening chapters—that the sins for which sacrifice can atone fall largely, indeed almost exclusively, into the category that we would call ritual. Overlap with the "ethical" (imagine a Venn diagram) is slight. Knowing failure by an individual Israelite to tell the whole truth in court, commission of fraud, petty thefts or deceptions—these are the closest the sacrificial system comes to ethics in chapters 5 and 8. Rape, murder, and other more serious crimes are dealt with elsewhere, as we would deal with them today, through civil and criminal law. Sacrifice thereby proclaims itself to be a *symbolic* system. It takes place—and places us—in the realm of purity and pollution. The system touches on the ethical only enough to remind us how distinct the two worlds otherwise remain—and that the former is meant to point to the latter. Ritual, we might say, touches life but is not life; it marks out bounds within which life can be lived well. It is a sort of art.[1]

We need that art because, no matter how complicated its details, it has one supreme advantage over life: *we can get it right.* I know that I will never live up to ethical ideals, even my own, in my relationships with other people. I will always "sin," which in Hebrew literally means missing the mark, falling short. I will not always be the spouse I should be to my wife, the father I want to be to my children. But I can get the Bach invention right, if I practice it long enough. I can leave a Yom Kippur *Ne'ilah* service, after twenty-five hours of following the prescribed ritual, with the precious sense of having at least done that much right. The ritual gives us a taste of rightness that is meant to inspire us to try to attain it outside the bounds of art as well.

Leviticus itself makes this move brilliantly when its laws of Sabbath observance lead to release of servants in the seventh year, to fallow years of sabbatical for the soil, and to the sabbatical forgiveness of debts. The discipline of ritual is designed to school us in the search for rightness and thereby to increase the chances that it will be achieved, that *we* will achieve it.

That is why the animals offered to God in thanksgiving or atonement or simple daily worship must be "perfect," without blemish. Indeed each ceremony as a whole must be exactly *comme il faut,* "as it must be," or else counts for naught, or even counts negatively and may lead to awful consequences (such as those that befall Nadav and Avihu in chapter 10). A hint of magic clings to this notion of ritual perfection—as if the cosmos hangs in the balance as one stands before the altar, and a human word or deed might actually alter the world for good or evil. Ritual is very much work, not play. Even today many people engage in ritual with a whiff of superstitious belief (or hope) that their symbolic actions can affect the way things work.

But that intent is not primary in Leviticus, I think, and is certainly not so for us today most of the time. What matters more is the model provided by ritual for the *perfection* we are meant to aim at in the rest of life, an ideal which it calls holiness. The animal has to be without blemish—the way we aim to be; it must be *whole,* just as ritual aims to engage the whole self: body and not just spirit; all five senses and not merely eyes or ears; the body in motion and not just at rest. Integrity, wholeness, is our goal too. This explains as well why Jewish ritual is rarely solitary. It almost always engages us in *communal performances,* connects us to other people in ways that words alone can never accomplish, reveals the pleasure of collective action. The ritual thereby increases the chance that we will join with fellow performers in undertaking the work to which the ritual jointly recalls us.

Sacrifices, like all ritual, are thus a serious game of make-believe. Ritual practices are of course not alone in this. Every legal system has its fictions. We decide that the rules will be X, Y, and Z, and when we encounter a situation that the rules cannot encompass we stretch them a bit, pretending we have not, to make them fit the reality to which they must be adequate. Parliamentary procedure can freeze the clock at a minute before midnight when the rules decree business be completed by twelve and the work to be done is not finished. My six-year-old engaged in a similar game when she pretended that one sofa was the ocean, another the playground up on shore, the carpet separating them a rocky beach. But we were barefoot, and the stones would hurt. How would we get from ocean to playground? By pretending a path had been paved among the rocks, or that we had left our beach shoes waiting at water's edge. Systems of ideas too have recourse to these twists and turns. As Max Weber said, they are like long division: a remainder is left over that does not come out even, which never seems to stop the builders of systems from trying.

Leviticus 16—the foundational text for Yom Kippur—assumes that God cannot abide impurity, as God cannot abide wrongdoing of any sort. Yet God has chosen, for reasons beyond the text's comprehension, to come down to earth in some sense and get involved in human history, and then to take up particular "residence" in the Israelite community. The problem urgently requires a solution. Life as a sinner in the presence of God would not be possible for us were it not possible to atone for our transgressions. (As it would not be possible for us to love other people without hope of their forgiveness: a connection not lost on the text.) And complete atonement in the real world, the ethical world, is impossible. The atonement must take symbolic form, so that we can see it happening, see ourselves attaining forgiveness in an unequivocal way that real life never allows, and erase wrongs that in the ethical sphere can never be entirely set right. This is the precious gift of ritual. What is done in its realm *can* be undone. Acts can take place—and then be erased, covered over: the force of the Hebrew root for atonement.

The Torah accomplishes the miracle of undoing the done by devising a series of concentric holy spaces. Aaron proceeds to the very center of the Tabernacle, the "Holy of Holies," entered only by him and only on this day and only after those spaces have been cleared of every other human being—and so of the sins their presence carries. Then he moves outward, sprinkling the blood of cleansing (made such by divine ordinance) on each succeeding space. So far so good.

But how will Aaron cleanse the camp as a whole? According to the symbolic logic established in the ritual, the camp too should be cleared entirely of sinful Israelites. All six hundred thousand of the males, not to mention women and children, should stand outside in the wilderness until Aaron's work is finished! That is not feasible. So the ritual adapts. The community loads its sins onto a goat, identical to one he had slaughtered as a sin offering, and sends it off to God-knows-where, carrying sins which—outside the human order, back in the natural elements of air and earth and fire and water—are as good as gone. Then, the sacred space purified, Aaron can shed his polluted garments and put on new ones, and the person who accompanied the goat outside the camp can do the same. All Israel can once more, via its priests, come near to God.

Lest they forget that what has transpired is "only ritual," the Israelites are ordered to "afflict their souls." This too is essential to their forgiveness. Later generations, in the absence of tabernacle or temple, made affliction—this time of body as well as soul—central to the day and substituted words of atonement for sacrifice. But the symbolic character of Yom Kippur remains in our day, as does its power. First we are to ask forgiveness from those we have harmed— the exchange of words repairing the damage, enabling us to go on— and then we are to devote just over twenty-four hours, evening to morning to evening, to the ritual of the day, composed entirely of words and other gestures. We are instructed to afflict the *body*, through fasting, lest the process be entirely invisible or entirely symbolic. We too are taught to begin on the inside, just as Aaron did, and work out. Finally, after a day of soul-searching, we too are meant to emerge convinced that we have done something real in the world and hoping that something in us has actually changed. We can't be certain of that. For we live in the world outside the walls of our sanctuaries, where nothing is certain, rather than in the world that ritual defines, the world of art, of clean lines and completions.

But neither can we live our everyday lives without ritual. We could not carry on relationships with those we love (and so hurt) the most were it not possible for words of apology and forgiveness to heal real wounds. It "is a pain" that forgetting to bring flowers on an anniversary can cause the grief it does, but that is to be expected when remembering the occasion can bring such happiness. *The symbols matter.* Recognition, anthropologist Erving Goffman has shown, is crucial to us even when it comes from people we barely know and hardly care about. All the more so do symbolic affirmations or rejections—mere words—heal or hurt us when they come from those we love.

Knowing that this is the case, it is hard for me to take seriously the arguments of purists who insist that all language and behavior must be spontaneous, and that ritual is therefore anathema to a thinking individual and should be left to "primitives" and children. Should we abandon our life-cycle rituals because their words are formulaic and their gestures stereotyped? Should I not have gotten married under a *huppah,* signing a *ketubah,* breaking a glass, reciting exactly the same blessings as millions of other bridegrooms over the centuries? Should we forego graduation ceremonies in our schools, or stop holding funerals and giving eulogies for our dead? Stop marking new years, and forego the occasion they provide for new resolutions and beginnings?[2]

I trust that I need not make the case for ritual to postmodern readers who no longer look to it for "literal truth" but rather for the meaning it offers precisely by not attempting literal truth. We all know the hurt that we inflict with words and the repair we effect with words. We all treasure the opportunity to start anew in each new year. Once we realize this, hold it fast in our attention, we are ready to appreciate Leviticus.

The vehicle of its repair of the world, the central symbol of its ritual, is sacrifice. Historians of religion differ in their interpretation of animal offerings. I find their arguments somewhat irrelevant to my purposes here. How can one establish that sacrifice in ancient Israel "meant" communion with God through sharing a meal, or atonement for sin by offering a gift of appeasement? Meant this to whom? What powerful activity means only one thing, in one way? What is *the* meaning of my going to synagogue on a given Sabbath, or buying my wife an anniversary present, or attending a farewell dinner for a retiring colleague? I prefer to look at sacrifice as a cultural language which once opened up all sorts of possibilities for meaning, just as every other cultural language does. Because sacrifice has long since ceased performing this work for us, I can't begin to say what Leviticus "must have meant" to ancient Israelites, though historical research into the cultures of the day provides valuable clues. It is far more important, I think, that I share the meanings to sacrifice—in the plural—that I find compelling in the present.

The first thing that the symbolic system of Leviticus conveys to me—and conveys better than any other discipline or art I know—is that everyday life, ordered in keeping with God's command, can be wonderfully rich and good *despite* the very real terror that haunts us (or me, at least) every day of life: the knowledge that one day death will take all we love from us, including life itself. In sacrifice I stand in front of the altar, my hand on the body of a throbbing animal about to die. I hear its scream and see its blood and smell its death, and I cannot but think: there but for the grace of God go I, today. One day it *will* be me. I scream too when I realize this, not cognitively but in my *kishkes,* my guts, from the depths.[3]

Leviticus reminds us of death repeatedly: not to make us morbid, or to have the prospect of the grave dominate our lives, but for exactly the opposite reason. It wants to help us *contain* death inside a life of order, richness, and meaning—and to contain not only our individual deaths but the threat posed by all of the world's pointless suffering and terrible chaos to the sacred order that the Torah seeks to build. Learn how to live, the text advises, in the awful presence of these many deaths and in the awesome presence of God. Do not focus on death to the point of obsession, and do not repress knowledge of it either, or pretend that death will not one day come to you. It will. It surely will. But do not forget that life is good. It can be beautiful and joyous. You can live it well. Ritual thus helps us face up to what is hardest, gives us the ability to stare it down, in the company of others who are doing the same and so sharing the strength we all need for holiness as for life.

It is for a similar reason, I think, that the injunction to love our neighbors as ourselves in chapter 19—a passage to which we shall return—is surrounded by warnings against forbidden sexual relations. Leviticus recognizes that sex is the master passion, indispensable to human relationships (not to mention creation), a source of pleasure and an aspect of love—but that it is also destructive of all too many marriages, friendships, and communities. We don't have to agree with the details of the book's approvals and disapprovals where sex is concerned in order to appreciate the havoc wreaked in our lives by sexual transgression. Leviticus is on target in this respect. Harassment is much in the news as I write. Adultery is *not* in the news—except when committed by celebrities—only because it is no longer rare but rather an ever-popular way for married men and women to hurt each other in search of fulfillments they cannot find at home.

Priests obsessed with purity and lineage of course had more reason than the rest of us to delimit sexual relationships carefully, but we all have reason enough. Ancients and moderns come together in matters of sexual sin. Communities then as now come apart because of them. If our lives are going to be holy, now as then, the test will not be days like Yom Kippur or the behavior of the saints among us but everyday relations, particularly with those closest to us and so most vulnerable to our desire and our hurt.

Leviticus nowhere seeks to repress sexual longing. It does not put a premium on ascetic renunciation of any sort. Quite the opposite. Its goal is to *contain* sexual drives within a sacred community—that is to say, a human community which despite inevitable sin aims at sacredness. Such a life must encompass not only holy times but every day (and night); not only the tabernacle but the entire camp of Israel, which is to be a "kingdom of priests and holy nation." The Torah is interested not only in the soul but in the most basic moments or functions of the animal body: eating, sex, reproduction, death. Eating is particularly important because it is the most direct relation we maintain to the rest of creation: a basic need and primal pleasure that routinely involves, if we are not vegetarians, the deaths of countless other creatures.

That is the point of the text's constant reminders to do this or do that, or avoid this or that, to make discriminations without end, "because I the Lord your God am holy." The concluding phrase does not provide authority so much as *motive*. Leviticus's God has created human beings with the intention of surrounding them, from birth to death, with meaning so palpable and rich that even the volatility of sex and the terror of death cannot undermine it. The order must be constructed in and through the things we do and do not eat, the people we do and do not sleep with, the forgiveness we extend to one another every day for the pain that we inflict every day. God can suggest this order but only we can construct it. Nor does God need it. We do.

At forty-something I am excited by this vision of the ordinary sanctified through attentiveness. I appreciate, in a way I could not a few years back, why Leviticus does not try to impose meaning cognitively, as Deuteronomy (or Plato) do when they seek to align each and every detail of law with a single overarching idea of the world. Such systems do not often work in my experience. The more comprehensive the attempt, the more glaring the failings. Too much of life will never fit. Too few of our concerns seem worthy or reflective of the grand ideas, and the match between ideas and actions is often tenuous at best. Human lives interest me far more at this point in life than ideas. Art and literature are more satisfying than philosophy. Concreteness appeals where abstraction cannot.

Leviticus's strategy is precisely to heighten ordinary experience, to take us higher, by focusing on the tastes and smells and desires that comprise life as we cannot but live it every day. Impose meaning at those innumerable points of entry to the sacred, the book urges. Start with the daily details that are so determinative of character (and therefore primary in neuroses): eating, washing, speaking, sex. Make discriminations there, and then work to see that moral discriminations follow. The book is positively relentless in its insistence that the highest end—love of neighbor—can be achieved only in and through focus on the smallest of details, particularly on those which (before therapy, at least) are often hidden from view. It immerses its readers in adult realia comparable to contemporary concerns such as mortgages and schools, retirement packages and wills—and urges that we work through these details to sanctification. The book knows of no other way to proceed. Leviticus wants us to find meaning and joy— or, where that is not possible, satisfaction—in the everyday world where we actually live, among the family, friends, and community who are best able to provide it.

The *collective* character of this project is crucial to Leviticus's purpose, and is, I think, another feature which draws the book (and us) ineluctably to ritual. The wonderful thing about ritual—another of its advantages over thought—is that it is out there, visible, in the space among individuals rather than inside any one of them. It possesses an objectivity that is never available to conscience or intention, a vividness that accrues only to what we can touch or taste or smell. As a result, ritual (when it works) not only prompts stirrings inside its participants but draws things from them as it draws them closer to one another. It elicits dancing of which participants might not have known they were capable. We find ourselves singing notes we would have thought beyond our range, are hugged in spontaneous embraces, cry unexpected tears. The emotion comes even when we know a particular ritual may elicit it, in fact may have been designed for just that purpose. For the ritual connects to something inside us not otherwise reached, in part because it connects us with other people and their depths. Often these are people who live in our vicinity but do not touch us on most occasions, are not touched by us.

This too seems part of the intent of sacrifice in Leviticus: a "bringing near," in the original Hebrew, an approach of the person bearing a living thing which is very close to the person, an offering of self, a presentation. Words seem a poor substitute for gifts of this sort—one reason we too insist on gifts, and not merely on words of congratulation, and why we often choose printed words or beautiful cards, rather than settling for mere spoken words. The latter are not sufficiently set apart from all the other words we speak for a million and one purposes. It is so hard to find the right words, when we have to compose them on the spot (though we appreciate it all the more when the effort succeeds). Far better, we decide, to step inside ritual words and enliven them with the fervor and originality of individual performance. We add scribbles to pre-made birthday or condolence cards, attend and perform plays, sing love songs that are well known. The very fact that the meaning is public, shared from the outset, assists us in using it to connect. Each person comes to the ritual with meanings and emotions already stored up and at hand. Our offerings are therefore all the more appreciated, and effective.

Every ritual exploits the power of that combination between a given script for enactment and the intention of individual performances. Jewish ritual time and again makes the relation between the two, the need for both, utterly central. At Passover it is even explicit. The Seder is not merely one of many rituals in the holiday cycle but the one which, as developed by the rabbis, seems paradigmatic of Jewish ritual as such. One sits down on a particular evening with family and friends around a table set with unusual objects: an egg, a shankbone, bitter herbs, unleavened bread. A member of the group recites the blessing over wine, *kiddush*, a symbolic marker which always functions in the Jewish ritual system to separate sacred from profane. The ceremony announces, in other words, that one is about to enter ritual space. Washing the hands—already clean—serves the same purpose. Then we embark on the reading of a text which begins by highlighting in four ritualized questions the symbolic differences between this evening and all other evenings: why matza rather than bread, bitter herbs rather than the usual vegetables, etc.? Lest we miss the point, the Seder text proclaims that "even were all of us wise, all people of understanding, all old and well-learned in the Torah, it would still be the duty to tell the story of our departure from Egypt. And whoever enlarges on the story it contains is to be praised."

Ritual action is not instrumental in character. We do not engage in it so as to accomplish something directly in the real world. We are not at the Seder in order to acquire skills or information, just as we do not wash our hands at the start of the Seder to get the dirt off. The ritual has other aims in mind. It quickly becomes apparent to us that only some of the questions we shall pose during the course of the meal have been scripted in the Haggadah. They will inevitably go far beyond the "four questions" with which the text begins. *Answers,* moreover, are never scripted with finality, because they cannot be. One has gathered around the table on this evening, surrounded by a particular set of symbols, so that one can ask *why* one has gathered around the table on this evening, surrounded by these symbols. "This matza which we eat: what meaning has it?" Had one not stepped into the ritual framework called Passover, one could not have asked these questions. Nor could one have learned that "answers," in this as every Jewish ritual, must come from each of us, singly and together, and must be given in the world outside the ritual as well: in the liberations we effect, in the redemptions we bring closer, in the narrow places we escape.

At Sukkot Jews are commanded to build fragile dwellings of our own construction, sturdy enough to stand up to the weather but open to the stars, and to eat and drink in them with friends and family surrounded by symbols reminding us of *why* Jews live inside distinctive constructions of meaning no less fragile and still more essential than a sukkah. At Shavuot Jews are meant to imagine themselves at Sinai, and to listen with new ears. The ritual of all-night communal study (instituted at first by medieval mystics and recently revived and made widespread) serves the aims of further clarity and concentration by setting the moment aside from the normal round of socializing and from the usual activities of the mind. Shabbat advances the same end every week, at once structuring time and helping us step out of time, the focus assisted by good food and warm fellowship: both of them commanded for the day, prescribed elements of the ritual, things we need and love but would not otherwise have taken the trouble to provide for ourselves. If kids are around, the celebration is complete.

One need not romanticize such rituals to attest their power. We all know that many artistic performances fall flat. The occupational hazard of ritual is that it can easily become mere repetition, rote performance. This often happens. To some extent it cannot be avoided. The tragedy is that all too many American Jews have never participated in a ritual which was *not* leaden, and have never been in a synagogue where the air is charged with excitement. They have known only dull repetitions from which the spontaneity had long since been drained. After a series of such lifeless rituals even a committed Jew can despair of finding more.

But then a moment comes—I myself witnessed several recently— when the full power stored up in the ritual is revealed. Someone in my *minyan* heard the recital of the Ten Commandments last year as if for the first time, and burst into tears. A friend watched his son circumcised, in the presence of his own father, and was overcome. A woman told me she had recently begun lighting Shabbat candles every week with her daughter—and it had changed her life. I am no longer surprised by such occurrences. The *New York Times* reports that sukkah-building is experiencing new popularity in America. Survey after survey confirms that Passover remains a holiday celebrated by many Jews who perform no other Jewish ritual. One of the most celebrated rabbis in America has instituted new rituals in his congregation marking life-cycle passages unknown to either Leviticus or the rabbis: college graduations, retirements, new careers. Jewish women are creating rituals and adapting others with an intensity that is inspiring. Some, I suspect, will prove permanent additions to the Jewish ritual repertoire.[4]

Activity in this realm has been truly staggering, and the response on the part of American Jews has been commensurate. Ritual performances, enlivened by new meanings and renewed appreciation of old ones, are once more serving as perhaps the single most effective vehicle for moving Jews inside the framework of tradition and extending the reach of the tradition beyond ritual into life. A single Shabbat experience is worth a hundred lectures. Leviticus knows this well. The task facing Jewish institutions in America today is therefore the one Jews have always confronted with regard to ritual: making it vital, involving Jews in its performances rather than permitting (or forcing) them to be mere audiences to happenings done on stage by others, getting adults and children alike engaged bodily in activities that provoke good questions and preclude easy answers. We know how to do all of this, even if we do not always do it well. And we have the comfort of knowing, when we fail, that the next opportunity is never more than a meal, or a Sabbath, away.

The Pleasures of Community

The ability of ritual to bring people together, tactilely and with power, has proven especially appealing to American Jews in recent decades, most likely because our society is so mobile and impersonal. We are uprooted repeatedly from those we love. The "nuclear family," if we live in one, and if it manages to stay together for more than the average of a few years, is surrounded largely with friends of recent acquaintance. Many people live entirely alone. The sense of community is attenuated. Workplaces are rarely supportive of emotional or existential needs. The result of these circumstances is that pressures are routinely placed on spouses and friends alike to provide fulfillments which in previous eras were readily available elsewhere, in the wider social networks of community. Our friendships suffer as a result. So too do our marriages and, some evidence suggests, our work.

The problem is compounded by the fact that we so rarely talk about it. The word "community" has become a buzzword cheapened by the frequency of use. How can one take the notion seriously when one hears every day about "the sports community" or "the business community," places built on the principle of competition, in which people are drawn together, if at all, only by shared interest? I know that I want something more from the word and the fact of community than that, and often seek in vain for its discussion, let alone for its realization. We are rarely treated to models of *any* kind of long-term relationships in American popular culture, friendships and marriages included. Extramarital affairs are everywhere on TV, and not merely on the soaps. Buddies abound. But marriages, good marriages, which stay whole despite the cracks? Adult rather than adolescent friendships? Adult conversations that go beyond one-liners? It is ironic that we are likely to decry the prohibitions of a book like Leviticus but seem utterly ascetic and self-denying when it comes to enjoying imagery of adult love: the day-by-day encounters through which friendships, marriages, and communities thrive and grow. Our popular culture shares and shapes little discourse of passion transmuted and heightened by common experience of the routine.

Robert Bellah and his co-authors in *Habits of the Heart* have argued convincingly that Americans share a "first language" about moral, social, and political matters that is heavily *individualist,* whereas the "second," more *communal* language derived from biblical and republican traditions is by and large latent and unused. As a result, they continue, Americans "have difficulty articulating the richness of their commitments. In the language they use, their lives sound more isolated and arbitrary than, as we have observed them, they actually are."[5]

I am suspicious of the latter claim. It might well be, as Herbert Gans has argued in *Middle American Individualism* (a polemical response to Bellah's book) that the language most in use reflects the predominant reality—that, in other words, Americans *are* by and large living the atomized lives to which their moral discourse attests.[6] Or it could be, as Michael Walzer has argued, that Bellah at once understates the degree of community which *does* exist and overstates the willingness of contemporary Americans to forego four sorts of mobility which most of us take for granted. These are (1) the *geographic* mobility that uproots us from family and friends, as we search for opportunity; (2) the *social* mobility that takes us far from the commitments and pursuits of our parents; (3) the *marital* mobility that not only permits divorce and remarriage but allows for unions across ethnic and religious lines (and, for some, now legitimately includes same-sex couples); and (4) the *political* mobility that has meant a loss of reliable loyalties to leaders, movements, or parties.

Walzer argues that we hold to certain truths as a society despite these four mobilities, that we can unite as a society around core ideals, and that some communal loyalties still compel us. Things will likely remain this way in any case, he believes, no matter what we say about community, because "there is no strong or permanent remedy for communal attenuation short of an anti-liberal curtailment of the four mobilities and the rights of rupture and divorce on which they rest."[7]

This challenge, I think, must be faced honestly by Jews like me who believe that our tradition and our communities *can* thrive in this country, and *do* thrive, only to the degree that they offer people a kind of ultimate meaning and a degree of serious community not readily available elsewhere. The need for community among Jews is as urgent as it is eternal. We are a small minority who require strong mutual connection if we are to preserve our rights, transmit our culture, and carry out our commitment to social justice. Without community, there can be no ritual reminders of what we are here to do; without ritual, there will be no community to fulfill the obligations to which our rituals point. American Jews have no choice but to strengthen group cohesion and commitment.

We will succeed in doing so only if we can reimagine Jewish community in forms that will prove acceptable to Americans such as myself who have been schooled on the "first language" of individualism, and who will therefore chafe for the reasons Walzer described at any surrender of autonomy. I know that I will not willingly forego any of my "mobilities" or options. But I also feel the need for a new language about community and suspect that would be true even were I not a Jew because of formative experiences in the sixties which made intense group relationships among men and women a principal source of life's meaning for me, and of life's pleasure. Because I am a Jew, community is uppermost in my mind, a longing well known to my heart since childhood.

Walzer's questions are thus all the more urgent. What do we really want, when we talk about Jewish community in America? And what if anything will Jews be willing to sacrifice in order to attain it?

My response begins with an unequivocal declaration of what I for one do *not* want: the return of any kind of Jewish community that has existed heretofore. The models applicable to our circumstances simply cannot be based upon those of previous eras. Neither the ghetto nor the shtetl has appeal. Nor are the *benefits* of inescapable community any longer accessible to us. The vast majority of Jews in this country will never spend their days—as Jews in ultra-Orthodox neighborhoods do still—within the confines of Jewish "gates and doorposts," ritually marked in ways that remind insiders and outsiders alike of where the boundaries lie. In the sacred order of Leviticus the limits of the Israelite encampment mark the limits of order as such. Beyond them there is only wilderness. That was not much less true for many Jews in actual communities throughout the ages, which were surrounded not by wilderness but by unknown and sometimes hostile Gentile populations with whom interaction, if it occurred at all, was often limited to business. Our circumstances, for better and for worse, are utterly different. I think the better far exceeds the worse in the present balance, and have no wish to alter it.

Yet Jewish texts—and still more Jewish history—do offer evidence of significant parallels to our own situation, parallels which in turn offer useful guidance as well as invaluable continuity. If we turn to the article on "community" in the *Encyclopedia Judaica*—a ready source—we learn for example that in Babylonia, in the talmudic period, *geonim* (rabbinic authorities) and exilarchs (communal leaders) worked together in uneasy coexistence. Local autonomy tended to be stronger than centralist institutions. The essay goes on to note that "the pattern of only one community board, or *kahal*, prevailed" up to the expulsion from Spain in 1492, but that afterward the "pattern of a community centered around its own particular synagogue re-emerged strongly in many areas and splintered the original community." The organized Jewish community tried to varying degrees in many eras, and with uneven success, to regulate the social, economic, and moral lives of its members. Migration to new areas and changes in circumstance led to "experiment in community living. Lacking the solid basis of long experience, [Jews] had to build from the foundation up. Great debates ensued among the handful of renowned scholars who valiantly strove to find precedents in talmudic law for solving communal problems."[8]

All of these are features familiar to us. Our religious and secular institutions compete far more than they cooperate. Turf wars between synagogues and federations, or synagogues and JCC's, are common. National organizations strain for the support of local affiliates, which chafe at the degree of control and "taxation" claimed. Rabbis and communal leaders preach about Jewish obligation—seeking to persuade, since they can no longer "regulate"—and are as a rule ignored. The intermarriage rate has not declined because of the communal hue and cry. Experiment, now as ever, is essential—and so too is debate over what "precedents in talmudic law" should be heeded, and what they mean.

My favorite talmudic passage on community is from *Tractate*

Baba Batra (page 7b). It begins with a text from the Mishnah (a code formulated at the end of the second century C.E.) which tells us that the residents of a courtyard may be compelled by the other residents to contribute to the building of a porter's lodge and a door for the courtyard. The residents of a city may be compelled by the other residents to pay for the building of a wall, gate, and crossbar. In both cases Rabbi Shimon ben Gamaliel, a noted authority, dissents. Not all courtyards require a porter's lodge. Not every city requires a gate. How long, the Mishnah continues, must a person live in a town to be counted a resident? Twelve months. But if he buys a house there he is counted as a resident at once.

The Gemara, commenting on the Mishnah, immediately queries these rulings. They seem to presume that building a porter's lodge is an improvement, a good thing. For the Mishnah, based on God's word in Torah, would never command something which might be a cause of evil rather than of good. Yet in this case the ruling might well lead to evil. "There was a certain man with whom the prophet Elijah used to converse, until he built a porter's lodge, after which he did not converse with him any more." The barrier kept the cries of the poor from reaching the residents inside, and so kept the poor from being fed and the residents from doing the mitzvah of feeding them.

It is striking that the Gemara, before it gets into the technicalities of who should pay how much (should the rich pay more? should those closest to the gate pay more?), is concerned that the good of self-protection not be the cause of harm. We are all too familiar with such dilemmas. They plague our society's attempts to curb crime and violence without grave harm to civil liberties. But several issues raised by the text are of still more immediate application.

American Jews too are engaged in deciding, as a community, what *boundaries* we need and how to erect them. This issue has been faced by significant segments of the Jewish people over the past two centuries and has resulted on the one hand in widespread acceptance of the opportunity to participate fully in Gentile societies when given a chance, and on the other in the creation of a separate State secured by international borders and the arms needed to protect them. The dilemma about boundaries faces the American Jewish community as a whole today as it worries about intermarriage, an anxiety exacerbated by shrinking numbers which have raised the specter of the community's disappearance.

Reform synagogues debate the role that should be permitted to the non-Jews among their members. Conservative synagogues wonder whether non-Jews should be allowed to be members—and whether any sort of standards should be "enforced" (via communal suasion) regarding personal observance. These questions of who is in and who is out are logically prior to debates over whether communal energy should be directed to bringing in new members—"outreach"—or to "inreach," serving those already involved or active.

Note too that it is *the group itself which is empowered by the Mishnah to decide* what its needs are with regard to doors and walls, subject of course to the constraints of Torah (explained in the previous chapter of this essay). The group can obligate its members by majority vote to contribute to the building of what is required. Rabbi Shimon ben Gamaliel may disagree, and may have a good reason for doing so, but the text vests the right of decision in the hands of the relevant community: courtyard or city. One is a member whether one likes it or not, has obligations which one may not have chosen to assume. This is not our situation in America today, of course. Members of every Jewish organization can leave it at any time, even if the fate befalling the Jewish people may not so readily leave them alone. But the vesting of authority in the community, subject to higher norms to which the Talmud will turn in a moment, remains.

Most usefully, perhaps, the text presents us with *concentric circles (or in this case rectangles) of belonging and obligation.* Members of a courtyard are in turn members of a city composed of multiple courtyards. That city, as we realize on subsequent pages of the Talmud, is part of a larger entity called the Jewish people, all of whom have responsibilities to one another. Nor do Jewish obligations end there. Gentile poor must also be fed. Gentile cities must be defended. The local face-to-face communities in which we may be involved are merely the core of wider circles of commitment. Every circle requires markers, "gates and doorposts," to signal and safeguard its distinctive identity. It also needs to be open to the outside.

That is the final point. *Walls we build have consequences both concrete and symbolic.* The most notable of these is captured in the Gemara's concern that a major substantive good, feeding the poor—a non-negotiable mitzvah in our tradition, the heart of Rabbi Akiba's dispute with the Roman general Turnus Rufus—might be compromised by empowering local communities to do what they have to do for their own self-defense. The message is both clear and pertinent. Anytime one creates structures that foster group life one brings people in—and keeps people out.

How can we build the walls high enough to define the distinctiveness of the group without building them so high that others, including people who belong inside (for example, Jews of a different class, or Jews who understand the Torah differently), are prevented or dissuaded from entering? How can we help people become secure in who they are without purchasing that security at the price of harm to others? And how can we avoid building the walls so high that Jews are reluctant to step inside the gates, lest they be locked in, as it were, against their will?

These dilemmas seem to me the givens of our situation, and return us directly to Bellah's vision and Walzer's cautions. My operative assumption, as I turn to the imagination of American Jewish community, is that whatever communities we construct will be *voluntary* rather than coercive. They will be *multiple* rather than unitary. And they will be *pluralistic* rather than monopolistic or dogmatic.

The *voluntary* character of our communities is their principal weakness, but it offers a potential strength as well. It means that Jewish communities will either speak to actual needs, articulate obligations which people recognize, provide fulfillments for which they yearn—or the communities will not elicit energies or shape lives. One dare not presume the existence of a "we" until it is established. Fictions of the sort one still finds in pious accounts of Jewish life— "We rise in the morning and say the prayer . . ." or "Every Jew of course believes that . . ."—will get us nowhere. The "American Jewish community" is itself a fiction of that sort. Nearly half of the born Jews in this country have nothing to do with the organizations of American Jewry at any given moment. Something like 20 percent will go through their entire lives without ever joining a Jewish institution. Synagogue membership has steeply declined, and only a tiny fraction of the community comes to synagogue on a weekly basis. Those who do join synagogues and organizations are a diverse group. No one leader speaks for them. Our efforts to build community must be adequate to their diversity. We must begin with what American Jews actually want or need and so would choose. The first step—rarely taken by synagogues—is to ask them.[9]

My belief, after countless conversations with Jews around the country, is that I am far from alone in wanting and needing more abiding connection with others and more ultimate meaning than our society and culture ordinarily provide. I treasure my options, my freedom to move in the four ways Walzer describes. I have moved from Philadelphia to Oxford to Jerusalem to New York to Palo Alto. I am currently involved in a variety of Jewish institutions, a member in several groups which aspire to be communities. Yet for all these changes and commitments there is one constant: I want my life to be bound up with that of other Jews in ties of tangible obligation as we together engage in serious dialogue with Jewish history and traditions. I seek such community everywhere I go, and choose to spend time and resources there with enthusiasm.

It is clear, too, that any community in which I am a member will never hold a monopoly on either my obligation or my affection. In this respect too—the *multiplicity* of affiliation—my own case seems typical. We all move in multiple worlds. Many Jews belong to a synagogue *and* a Hadassah chapter, or give to Federation *and* the New Israel Fund. This is still more true as we extend *Baba Batra*'s concentric rectangles of belonging outward beyond the Jewish world; indeed, for many of us, non-Jewish commitments are at or near our very center. The Jewish world—and certainly the Jews who belong to it—should rejoice in, rather than bemoan, the plurality of competing organizations, causes, and groups that dot our landscape and solicit our dollars. There is no better way to keep Jews Jewish, or to keep organizations responsive to actual and felt needs. The same would hold true of membership in multiple communities of the more serious sort that I am urging.

For activism in one area tends to correlate with (rather than preclude) activism in another. Jewish concerns do not crowd out one another, or crowd out American or human concerns. They are all of a piece for a generation at home in America and increasingly, one hopes, at home in Judaism as well. Nor is the *quality* of a person's experience of Judaism measured by the relative *quantity* of time devoted to it. The two are connected, of course. A Jewish identity contracted in time and space to an hour or two spent in the synagogue once a month, or a meeting of an organization once every other month, will likely not prove viable. But neither is all time of equal significance. The fifteen or twenty minutes a family spends lighting Shabbat candles Friday night, saying *kiddush* and the *motzi* (blessing before the meal), singing Shabbat songs around the table, are not equal in weight to the twenty minutes, or two hours, spent after a normal meal watching TV or talking on the phone. The ritual has power. One steps into another realm with the sacred.

There are no hard and fast rules here. No one knows how many hours of "Judaism" per week are "enough," or how much time must be spent in a community for it to be defined as such. The members of each group will know when their ties to one another and their encounter with texts and traditions are serious. Rewards for investment are apparent.

There is an immediate and practical consequence of this approach. Synagogues gloating at the belated recognition by federations that "continuity" requires content, that Jewish survival alone is not enough of a goal to ensure that survival, cannot claim in response that they constitute the sole "gateway" to Jewish meaning in this country, let alone the sole Jewish community of substance. Synagogues already cannot claim a monopoly on Jewish education—far from it. Day schools are teaching an ever-growing percentage of Jewish children, while adult learning—which seems to grow exponentially every year—takes place in secular organizations such as Hadassah and the American Jewish Committee, in JCC's, and under the auspices of organizations established for the purpose, such as CLAL and the Wexner Heritage Foundation, as much as or more than it takes place in synagogues.

Nor, however, should federations mistakenly believe that they alone constitute or bear responsibility for the community as a whole. Synagogues too are a major address for community, when they understand that this is what their members need and want. The same is true for other projects and organizations. Community can happen, does happen, wherever Jews are brought together time and again around causes which bring them into dialogue with Jewish tradition as well as with one another. Cooperation among synagogues, and between synagogues and federations, would be of inestimable value in facilitating more substantive community.

That brings us to my third operating assumption: *pluralism.* The fact of Jewish diversity will continue to be inescapable in this country. Jews are too different from one another to be satisfied with one formula for communal expression, and too free in their options regarding affiliation to settle for any community that demands suppression of other aspects of themselves or disengagement from other affiliations. Religious denominationalism—the need, as the old joke goes, for every Jew to have two synagogues: one to pray in and one which he or she would never set foot in—is the least of it. Needs flowing from age and gender vary tremendously. So do interests and passions that cut across those divides. We cannot predict what will excite Jews and link them in coming years either to each other or to the tradition. We do know, however, that Jewish renewal in this country, for all that it has been aided by resources flowing "downward" from central federation coffers and the offices of national organizations, has been very much a grass-roots affair. Whether we are speaking of women's groups, activities to feed the hungry, the outreach efforts of HABAD, or movements to protect the environment or foster spiritual growth, we are dealing with authentic needs so powerful that they have rather quickly found institutional expression and in the process transformed the contours of American Jewish life.

One can only hope that our various organizations will come to see diversity not just as a fact but as a good, and will extend the mutual respect which has often been lacking (and not only from the Orthodox side by any means). Actual cooperation is at present almost as rare—despite obvious opportunities and advantages.

With the ground rules of our pursuit in place, we can proceed now to a sketch of the several sorts of Jewish community which seem desirable and possible within the constraints of our society, our culture, and our own profound ambivalence about the surrender of personal autonomy. My aim here is to respond to both of Walzer's questions at once: to say *what* I would like the Jewish community to be, and *why* I think substantial numbers of Jews would be willing to sacrifice resources and autonomy in order to build such a community and be part of it. Jewish community as I imagine it must exist on three levels simultaneously.

Leviticus: Ritual and Community

It must in the first instance be *local: face-to-face,* or as near to it as possible. Community can be built only from the ground up, on the basis of clear and present needs, and will be held together primarily by the cement of personal connection linking each person and his or her *re'a,* or neighbor—the one whom Leviticus 19 commands me to treat as I would want to be treated. In our circumstances the *re'a* is generally not the person who literally lives next door but someone who has been "brought near" by shared commitments.

This is the kind of community found in *havurot*: small groups, organized around prayer, study, and/or family celebrations of sabbaths and holidays, which formed in major American cities and college towns during the late sixties and seventies. I first found an answer to my own yearning for Jewish community in a *havurah* on the Upper West Side of New York, in this case a *minyan* (prayer group) that began to meet in the late seventies. Many women of my acquaintance have found similar satisfactions in women's *minyanim* or *Rosh Hodesh* (literally: "first of the month") groups devoted to fellowship, prayer, study, and the creation of new rituals and midrash. A small synagogue, an individual chapter of a national organization, the set of activists in a local federation, or even an entire small Jewish "community" (in the usual sense) can likewise constitute a face-to-face community of the sort that I have in mind here. All are larger than individual friendships or nuclear families and yet smaller than our cities, ethnicities, religions, or national organizations. Most include both men and women, and members of several age-groups, though others are more narrow in this regard. But all, unlike "lifestyle enclaves" convened for a single purpose, unite people across a variety of settings via a set of common interests which crisscross as much as the networks of friends which the groups facilitate.

The key point with any such local community, then, is not the specific content of its activities (i.e., prayer, shabbat meals, study, consciousness-raising, social justice work) or the form taken by the group (synagogue, organization, fellowship, etc.) but that the framework facilitate face-to-face relationships which in turn become a vehicle for the abiding personal connections that over time generate communal norms. Existing Jewish communities in the strong sense that I am advocating already influence their members' lives in a number of areas. Neither curtailment of autonomy nor preaching the virtues of certain behavior is involved. The influence comes from trust, and time required to build trust is invested in large measure because of the sheer pleasures of living in regular contact with people who share one's commitments, of watching them and their children grow, of "being there" for them and having them "be there" in turn at times of stress and times of celebration alike.

There is every evidence that more Jews would place their people's traditions at the core rather than the periphery of their lives if they too were part of strong face-to-face communities. The institutions which currently work best in promoting Jewish identity in America are those which transmit Jewish meaning in the midst of palpable community: Jewish camps, Israel experiences, and day schools. The synagogues which succeed are likewise those which give people a sense of connection to others. There is surely no surprise in that. We all have enough impersonal and bureaucratic institutions in our lives, and do not need yet another one in the form of a synagogue, which would in that case offer no "sanctuary" whatsoever from the chaos outside. Why should a Jew step into its space on a regular basis, let alone pay the formidable annual dues?

Jews will and do, however, respond to experiences of genuine community by returning for more, often with offerings of time or other resources in hand. The members of such groups, in fact, often decide together to *enlarge* the area of their shared activity—building outward from whatever point of origin they have made their center— and this in turn involves still greater sacrifice, offered readily. Day-care centers lead to *havurot* for holiday celebrations. *Minyanim* spin off study groups. Face-to-face Jewish communities in contemporary America have grown up around schools and geriatric centers, food co-ops and professional organizations, as well as in synagogues, organizations, and independent *havurot,* and have likewise built outward in a variety of directions: schools, homeless shelters, holiday celebrations, environmental work.

The second level of Jewish community—the outermost concentric rectangle in *Baba Batra*'s model—is *"global": that of American Jewry or the Jewish people as a whole.* Local Jewish communities have such a great effect on Jewish lives—and excite such powerful ambivalence—because they are never merely local. Each represents the totality of Jewish history and tradition; signifies the covenants of fate and destiny; speaks in a voice bearing the resonances of parents, conscience, and God.

Every Jew with eyes open to the history of this century and basic knowledge of previous centuries knows that Holocaust and Israel, no matter how far away they might seem, involve them rather directly. Hitler's reach extends to psyches never exposed to Rashi or the *siddur*. So does the State of Israel, particularly when the news about it shown on television is troublesome. However, in this case too curse and blessing go hand in hand; what has weakened the community is also potentially a source of strength. Although many Jews are no doubt in flight from the weight of their people's history and the quandaries it poses, most Jews also feel considerable pride at their people's achievements over the centuries and today. Counting the Jews among Nobel prize winners and other lists of celebrities is a well-known Jewish sport. The benefits, real and imagined, of attachment to one's people and all it stands for are substantial. And they are near at hand: as close as a local synagogue or chapter of Hadassah. Involvement in the amazing projects the Jewish people have "on the ground" in this world is likewise easily purchased. One can help to rescue Jews from Ethiopia or the former Soviet Union, join in the building of Israel, help provide jobs and vocational training to people in need of them, feed the poor, house the homeless.

The global level of Jewish community unites Jews in the covenants of fate and destiny alike. It also lends support—"plausibility" as precious as that secured on the local level—to the conviction that the ideals expressed in Jewish texts, rituals, prayers, and fund-raising appeals are not mere rhetoric or self-important puffery. Torah still matters in the world. National or international conventions of Jewish activists such as the General Assembly of the Council of Jewish Federations represent powerful testimonies in this regard. When held in Israel, they take on the character of pilgrimage. One witnesses with one's feet, in the journey to the common center. Association with the Jewish people can provide as much meaning as a person could wish for in this life, and sometimes more than one can handle. Hence the ambivalence exposed in so many interviews with American Jews—and familiar to membership chairs and fund-raisers for every Jewish organization.

The sense of global community is all the more precious, I suspect, because the Jewish community is in other respects so obviously fractured on *every* level. This Jew will not sit down with that one; this Jewish movement will not recognize the other's Judaism as the genuine article. The covenant of fate singling out Jews for persecution has all too often not led to cooperation in pursuit of the covenant of destiny but precisely the opposite. It is as if, unable to punish their enemies, Jews take out their anger on one another, accuse each other of vile treachery, invoke what is highest in their eyes—God and Torah—to justify behavior that, when others sink to it, they recognize as the lowest. Jews complain to me about the lack of Jewish unity constantly—and respond warmly whenever unity is perceived. The need for it seems visceral, a response to centuries of diaspora and to this century's particular horrors. All the more reason for attraction to positive experiences of Jewish peoplehood. Jews in my experience often emerge from them energized and ready for action, and return for more such experiences at the first opportunity.

This points to the importance of the final level of community, which we might call *"middle-range"* because of its size, scope, and function. I refer to groups which offer continuing encounter with segments of the Jewish people larger than a local community but smaller and more frequently accessible than "American Jewry" or "world Jewry" as a whole. Middle-range communities can arise in larger synagogues, regional federations, cultural organizations, or political causes. Their members see each other's faces regularly, though they do not know most participants or even their names. Middle-range communities, less homogeneous than local communities, must also embrace and accommodate a wider variety of interests. It is not only possible but convenient for a person to belong to multiple communities of this sort simultaneously, whereas face-to-face communities tend to be more demanding and therefore more exclusive. This does not prevent enduring ties of affection (though probably not love) from developing over time at the middle-range as well. Community is built through shared labor for the same cause, and nurtured by the discovery that, only five minutes into the first encounter, one can abandon small talk in favor of short-hand conversation about things that matter. Members soon begin to attend each other's weddings and funerals. Shared obligation leads to overlapping networks of affection.

Many synagogues and organizations have recognized that they serve their members in large part by functioning as middle-range communities. Stated organizational goals or prayer services are, from the members' point of view, often secondary. To cite one example, educational efforts are now commonplace in organizations such as

Hadassah and the American Jewish Committee, even though study is far from either group's original or primary purpose. Jewish learning has proven popular to the members because it joins them to one another at the same time as it links them to their tradition, without requiring assent to any particular belief or observance of any particular ritual. Organizations respond positively to this interest because study not only cements their members' loyalty but legitimates the organizations' role as a carrier of the Jewish past, a constituent of the Jewish people.

A similar example is provided by the "Maimonides" and "Cardozo" societies which have recently sprung up across the country to bring together Jewish physicians or lawyers. Participants are grateful for the opportunity to give public expression to the connection they themselves make between their Jewishness and their professions. For many, the occupational niche they occupy is not merely a sociological function of the opportunities available to Jews in twentieth-century America but the result of moral commitments which they believe emerge from Jewish tradition.

Jewish cyberspace is emerging as yet another middle-range community; collaborations among Jewish artists and conventions of scholars in Jewish studies can serve a similar function. All feature conversation, formal and informal, over the direction of Jewish life and Jewish traditions—and thus become *part* of that life, a vehicle for those traditions.

Some would argue that the attempt to "grow" Jewish communities in America on all three levels—local, global, and middle-range—is objectionable because it is not spontaneous. Is this not the sort of social engineering for which Mordecai Kaplan was roundly criticized over half a century ago? Kaplan is, I confess, the "presiding presence" of this analysis. He well understood the importance of "reconstructing" the American Jewish community, and his success in doing so was, I believe, perhaps his greatest achievement. Kaplan's mistake was in imagining the Jewish community at once too narrowly and too broadly. He tended to dismiss communal forms and commitments which he believed incompatible with modernity or America, even as he urged a unified organizational structure insufficiently flexible to accommodate the features of voluntarism, multiplicity and diversity which to me are givens.[10] There is no reason that the various organizations and causes of American Jewry should be united under one central authority, and many reasons they should not, just as there is no need for the Jews who sit at the same Passover table or join in a Hanukkah celebration to agree on what those holidays mean, let alone to affirm unanimously that the Red Sea actually parted or the oil really lasted for the eight days of the Temple's cleansing.

The strength of community, as of ritual, lies in its potential to bring people together despite differing backgrounds and beliefs: to take them out of themselves into a space "between" and then return them to themselves, to their private spaces, transformed. As Kaplan himself learned from the great sociologist Emile Durkheim, it is the *experience of this transformation,* and not the particular content associated with it, that confers power on ritual and community. The experience of Jewish community, the sense of lived connection to the covenants of fate and destiny, is what brings Jews back for more of the same. It roots them in place despite all the mobilities that Walzer described and bonds them more tightly to the Jewish people and Jewish traditions despite their unwillingness to sacrifice autonomy or foreclose options. The magic does not work for all Jews in this country and never will. Given its success thus far, however, the aim of actively involving another 10 percent of the community over the course of the next decade or so—half a million Jews—does not seem to me at all unrealistic. The resultant transformation of the community would be beyond measure.

Loving the Good, Together

Perhaps the single most memorable passage in Leviticus, a high point of the book for virtually every reader, and certainly the best-known of the Torah's commandments, comes in verse 18 of chapter 19: "Love your neighbor as yourself; I am the Lord." The section begins with God telling Moses to command "the whole Israelite community" to "be holy," as God is holy. A code very similar to the Ten Commandments follows, enjoining respect for parents, forbidding idolatry, and prohibiting theft and deception. In keeping with Leviticus's emphasis upon correct ritual performance, regulations regarding sacrifice are integral to this list, inseparable from the ethical commandments to which they point. "You shall not insult the deaf, or place a stumbling block before the blind. You shall fear your God: I am the Lord." Hatred of "kinsfolk" in one's heart is prohibited right after unfair judgment, both being destructive of community. "Reprove your kinsman. . . . Do not take vengeance or bear a grudge. . . . Love your neighbor as yourself. I am the Lord."

Two implications of the command to love are directly relevant to our discussion. The first is the *behavioral* connotation of the command. It does not order a certain feeling inside the self, but (like the command countering hatred of one's fellows in one's heart) demands behavior that occurs in the relations between selves. The literal force of the Hebrew is directional: love is *toward* the neighbor, moving the self in his or her direction, bringing the two closer. As a general rule the Torah has a great deal to say about *interpersonal relations* and almost nothing to say about *intrapersonal feelings*. Its focus is the objective realm which people share, the rituals which bring them together, and the communities they build. Law is meant to guide these pursuits. It cannot and does not try to regulate the heart or the mind.

And yet, as this passage reveals, the Torah is not indifferent to the *passion of community*. Leviticus spends a good deal of time, as we have seen, seeking to channel rather than to extirpate desire, to sanctify rather than proscribe the carnal aspects of humanity. It would be surprising if it did not also recognize, as it does here, that passion flows into and out of group life. The rabbis too testified to this eloquently, most notably in Pirke Avot. Look in particular at 6:1, apparently a medieval addition to the tractate, which builds on preceding verses to reach this climax:

> Rabbi Meir said: He that occupies himself in the study of the Torah for its own sake merits many things, and, still more, is deserving of the whole world. He is called friend, beloved, lover of God, lover of mankind, and it clothes him with humility and reverence and fits him to become righteous, saintly, upright and faithful. . . . And it gives him kingship and dominion and discernment in judgment; to him are revealed the secrets of the Torah, and he is made like a never-failing spring and a river that flows ever more mightily. . . .

Note Rabbi Meir's extravagant language and its emphasis upon the eros of those who fill their days with Torah. This is a passionate statement of the reward stored up for lovers of Torah, a reward conceived in overflowing terms of love and joy. The chapter's third verse accounts somewhat for the sense of gratitude and obligation alike.

> He that learns from his fellow a single chapter or a single halakha or a single verse or a single expression or even a single letter, must pay him honor (*kavod*). . . . And honor is nothing else than Torah, for it is written, "The wise shall inherit honor" and "the perfect shall inherit good" and "good" is nothing else than Torah, for it is written, "For I give you good teaching, forsake not my Torah."

We have all learned something from our fellows, have all received Torah from them. Torah is the weight we have in this world, what keeps us from being blown away with the breeze, what gives us dignity and honor. *Kavod* descends to earth from a divine source, circulates among us, and only thus ascends once more. The obligation and need to give it in turn to others derives from the knowledge that our parents had it to give us only because they too had received it, in necessarily imperfect transmission, as had our friends, and so on in an infinite chain.

The circulation of love generates more love; the place this happens is called community. Mishnah 6 goes on to teach that Torah is acquired in no less than forty-eight ways, among them: love; loving God; loving humanity; loving rightness, reproof, and the straight and narrow. Love, in the first mishnah a *reward* for Torah, is in this verse its *prerequisite*. The circle is endless. Hence (mishnah 9) the urgent need to live in a place of Torah, so that one can retrace the circle's path, and so complete it.

It is not Leviticus's way—or the rabbis'—to philosophize about love or anything else for that matter. Systematic statements about love are not to be found in the biblical corpus, though an entire book, Song of Songs, is devoted to poetry full to overflowing with the passionate desire of man and woman for one another.[11] But if the Torah were to define love, it might well do so somewhat as Plato does in the *Symposium,* a dialogue about love significantly embedded, as the rabbis would want it to be, in *aggada* or story. The definition comes after numerous and sundry speeches around the banquet table in praise of love, most of which employ the hackneyed conventions to which we ourselves normally resort when talk turns to love. Then the goddess Diotima enters the discussion via Socrates' narration—she would be a wise woman in the Talmud, or her words would be attributed to one of the rabbis most at home in passion: Resh Lakish, perhaps, or Akiba himself—and provides a definition that I find utterly arresting. "Eros," she says, "is love of having the good for oneself always."

It strikes us at once that love is defined in terms of love, and defined in the first instance as *desire*. A recent translation by Alexander Nehamas renders the phrase as "love is wanting to possess the good forever."[12] Love is desire for the good. Eros, we might say, is always assertive in the Greek—ever agitated, on the move, full of eagerness and energy. In Plato's theory, amenable to the spirit of Leviticus, love begins with desire and never really leaves it behind. Eros is never, as we would say, merely Platonic: never "pure" or untouched by multiple and powerful longings. Plato, like Leviticus, recognizes the various objects of desire and the many forms that desire can take. Sex, we should note, is only one (though hardly the least) of them. Nor is beauty merely incidental as cause (and effect) of desire. It even enters the dialogue bodily in the person of Alcibiades—as sexual desire pervades the pages of Leviticus, bursting forth from the many prohibitions to which it gives rise. Passion is the beginning of love for Plato, and not only the beginning. But it is not the end. Like Leviticus, he seeks to direct desire, to sanctify it.

Love is desire *for the good*. This means that love is not to be reduced to desire. Even in sex (and by analogy in other desires) what we want is often not merely a body with which to satisfy the body's urges for a brief moment but substantial human connection, intimacy, union, fulfillment. A decision on this point seems crucial. Our consumer culture sells nearly everything through sex. It titillates and arouses us at every turn, attempting to convince us that sex is not only more important than previous cultures had believed but uniquely bound up with personal fulfillment and authenticity. *They* repressed, denying this centrality to sex. *We* are honest. Leviticus seems to maintain, as does Plato, that we can't speak truly about love without owning up to the obsession, the craziness, the ecstasy, the lovesickness. But desire is not all—and the obsession, the ecstasy, the lovesickness do not stem only from desire. There is more to it.

This "more," Plato maintains, again in keeping with Leviticus, concerns *the good*; where friendship and especially marriage are concerned, what we love most is a clear and present image of the good. We affirm to the friend or the beloved, and affirm this not only because of the pleasure they bring us, "You are good. You have your life on course. Stay as you are. I want you as you are in my life. Loving you is therefore good for me, brings good my way."

That is why the good is *for oneself.* Both texts presume a powerful desire for connection to the good at work in all of us. It seems inseparable from our desire to know the essential truths about existence and is perhaps rooted in the desire to cleave to existence, to walk the way that (as Buber put it) *is* life.[13] Straying from the way, letting go of life or truth, is sin—from which Leviticus is desperately concerned to save us. Walking the path is holiness. It stretches before each person, in every situation. Those we love help us not to miss the path, by offering us the opportunity to have the good in our lives the only way it gets there on a regular basis: affixed by people who live it in our proximity and draw it forth from us. We find or lose it daily together with those we love. In sex too we taste another's goodness, satisfy the need not to search alone, join forces against the nothingness, create a moment of power and beauty that *is,* has weight, seems true. I am grasping now, as we grasp in our love-making, wordlessly, and as Plato too grasps in phrases such as "begetting and birth in the beautiful." He, like Buber, seems intent on expressing the double paradox of a desire *for* the good that in turn channels desire *toward* the good, raising it higher.

We want this good, finally, *always*—the word I most treasure in Plato's definition of love. Love is the desire to have the good *always.* I confess I've always heard the word inside as I loved, as I hear it echoed in Leviticus's refrain, "I am the Lord"—that which is not mortal, that which grounds the person who obeys the commandment to love the neighbor in a way that does not end. We've all felt similar longings, I suspect, perhaps even shouted them out loud. We want the moment of sexual union never to end. We want the conversation to go on forever. Why can't community abide rather than dissipate? Death stands all about us. So does boredom, gray normality. Let love counter all this, be for always!

Plato makes no claim that love is "strong as death," a declaration appropriate to the love poems of the Song of Songs but unsuited to philosophy. The truth is that love cannot keep death at bay or bring the dead back to life. Leviticus knows this as well, and will not permit us to evade the fact. But Plato, like Leviticus, suggests that in love we taste something eternal, enter a realm which is not subject to time. Love constitutes our most palpable experience of transcendence. It carries the conviction of transport to a More, a larger possibility for existence than we are accustomed to consider. The soul is touched and quickened. The spirit rises and soars. I take this to be the meaning of Buber's avowal that every I-Thou experience provides a gateway to the Eternal Thou. "Extended, the lines of relationship intersect in the Eternal Thou. Every single Thou is a glimpse of that."

Shall we believe this or shall we not? In what sense shall we believe it? This is the question all of us face when determining how to allot our time, and particularly when deciding whether it is worthwhile to venture forth from the surer domestic space of love to public spaces, communities, which rely even more than marriage upon *obligation* to sustain relationships in the interstices separating moments of actual passion, of "real love." All of us know by the time we are adults, or should, that marriage and romance are not the same. Any sociologist can tell you that communities built on affect, much less on eros, are notoriously unstable. The mix of obligation and affection on which community (like marriage) relies is a surer recipe for stability.

But Leviticus and Plato, seconded in this respect by Buber, directly challenge the suspicion ingrained in many moderns that love is *generally* to be doubted, wherever we encounter it, and that the More to which it leads us is *always* to be denied. Such suspicion follows the Freudian principle that if we appear to be getting what we want in this life we must be deceiving ourselves. Things "too good to be true" cannot be true. We want to conquer death, says the skeptical voice, and so the desire to have the beloved for ourselves *always* is at once comic, pathetic, and sweet—but surely has no truth behind it. Could it be, in this most important of all cases, that we have a chance of actually getting what we want? Could love actually purchase the good for all of us, and for always? If so, promise and fulfillment would in love really come together—a precise and classic definition of a miracle.

I do not know, of course, whether this miracle is true. All I can say here, as in the previous chapter, is that I too—like Plato, like

Leviticus—sense God's presence in certain precious but fleeting moments, many of them bound up in experiences of love, some of them in the experience of community. In Buber's terms, we enter an I-Thou realm that arises out of and inhabits everyday experience and yet opens a gateway to the Eternal.[14] Love, we might say, is more directly touched than the ordinary by God. It is, in this sense at least, *of* God. That is why the Torah can use the same word when commanding us in God's name to "love the Lord your God" as it does in the not much less difficult and not much clearer command to "love your neighbor"—and why, perhaps, it commands us to love "*et*" God in the Hebrew, "*with* God," but "*le*" or "*toward*" the neighbor. We are circulating a good that did not begin with us, and will not end with us.

That is why it was so important for Buber that we not picture love as a feeling inside individual selves but rather as a fact, an achievement, among them—the reason why he more than any other twentieth-century Jewish thinker articulated the passion of Jewish community. Buber was no partisan of mere form, whether in religion or in love. He detested institutional rigidity, and to my mind exhibited far too little tolerance for the fixed routines necessary to sustain the friendships and communities he craved. Buber also had notoriously little patience for ritual. But he was determined that we provide the personal, cultural, and societal supports needed for serious relationships to flourish. Without community, love could not develop and the spirit could not soar. Inside community, however, the lines of relation have the chance of reaching all the way from one point on the circle to another, and, when "extended," of meeting in the Eternal Thou.

If community does its job, "always" is not only the endpoint of desire for the good but the time and place of its opportunity: the everyday. Were I a poet schooled in the teachings of Leviticus, I would try to sing of "ordinary evenings" in New York, Jerusalem, and Palo Alto as well as New Haven. I would want to capture the peace of a Shabbat dinner table; the pleasure of friendships built up year by year at the Passover table; the satisfactions even arguments can provide when they take traditional form: how many plagues were delivered in Egypt and how many on the Sea, how high should one build the walls and gates of Jewish communities, how much energy should be devoted to "inreach" as opposed to "outreach", how much effort should be spent on Jewish needs and how much on the larger worlds in which we move. Such quarrels "for the sake of heaven" testify to the existence of the shared community and commitment which shapes them, and is shaped by them.

Such pleasures of the everyday, for all the routine trouble and inevitable dullness intermixed with them, and the many evils that continue in the world, likewise visible every day, enable one to say, "Dayyenu. It is enough for us." Attentive to the foreground, part of a community which shares it, we know what it is to want only more of the same, and have a sense of what it might mean to live inside a sacred order. If I only had the words, I too would sing the praises of this everyday mightily and would not contradict those who discern in it, with keener vision than I yet possess, the activities of the Most High.

4

⚬✖⚬

Numbers

POLITICS IN THE WILDERNESS

Numbers, surely not by accident, is the least disciplined of the Torah's five books. As befits the subject matter—wilderness wanderings, complaint and rebellion, desire run rampant—the book positively sprawls. No overarching order here: no Levitical rhythms of sacrifice and tabernacle, no pastoral tales of faith and betrothal, no Exodus, and certainly no Sinai. Instead we find the troubled mixture of covenant and normalcy which marks all of Jewish history. Promise beckons to the people clearly from across a narrow river. They want desperately to attain it. But they want so many other things as well: the leeks and onions they remember eating in Egypt, the water that God can make gush forth from rocks, the power that Moses and Aaron seem to have monopolized for themselves. "Welcome to the real world," the book seems to say. "It is not a sanctuary. If you want to change and sanctify it, come and get your hands dirty. Get power and use it wisely. It's time for politics."[1]

Jews have always cared inordinately about politics. We have had no choice but to care about it, for reasons rooted both in *normalcy* and in *covenant*.[2] The interests of a perpetual minority—first concern of normalcy—demand constant vigilance. Rights and freedoms garnered from the powers that be must be protected. No less, the *raison d'être* of the Jewish people—arguably not merely an ideal but what has kept Jews alive for two millennia against all odds—is the prophetic demand that justice sit at the very top of the Jewish communal agenda. A right social order—the goal of covenant—is not simply one among many things Jews are meant to strive for but the essential thing, the completion of creation for which God "elected" Israel in the first place. When Jews fail to carry out this command, as they often do, of course, the tradition is unsparing in its condemnation. Normalcy—the world as it is, was, and shall be—is for the Torah raw material meant to be raised up, sanctified, redeemed, according to the covenant.

As a consequence of that unchanging demand, the nature and goals of Jewish politics must change repeatedly, and have done so over the centuries. Normalcy requires constant adaptation to new circumstances—and so too, therefore, does covenant, which must be imposed on the only reality there is. Never has the need for change been more apparent than now, when the Jewish situation in both America and Israel—the two foci of this chapter—is utterly without precedent.

In America, Jews enjoy full participation in the larger society, a degree of attainment and at-homeness new to Jewish history. The vast majority do not regard themselves, as almost all Jews did until a century or two ago, as "temporary residents" in transit to Zion, their only real home. They do not sit waiting for God's messiah to take them there. Nor need Jews rely, as they still do in some countries of the world, upon "court Jews" or other notables to plead their case before Gentile powers. With full benefit of Emancipation, and ample use of the influence that has come with economic clout and other achievements, American Jews today work with allies (and against opponents) through the normal democratic process of give and take, bargaining and leverage. Like other groups, they act both to protect communal interests (variously defined) and to pursue (one version or another of) a distinctive societal vision. The community's political skills are by this point quite refined, and justly admired. Its attainments are enviable, even if still haunted by the fear that America will not prove as much an exception to previous diaspora history as Jews might wish.

Israeli Jews, possessing actual sovereignty over a piece of territory for the first time in two millennia and maintaining one of the finest armies in the world, of course enjoy a far greater degree of control over their society, economy, and polity. "Normalization"—a primary goal of Zionism from the outset—has to that extent been achieved. Its consequence is that Israelis practice a still more revolutionary

Jewish politics than American Jews and face more of a challenge in fulfilling covenantal duties. It is one thing to call for social justice in the name of Isaiah, or cite the Torah's demand to "seek peace and pursue it," or cry out with Leviticus against oppression, when one has little or no power to act on such demands, lacks influence sufficient to see that they are met, and bears no direct responsibility for the outcome of decisions once they are made. Jewish politics is quite another matter when it weighs competing needs or goods, uses state power to counter other groups and their traditions, justifies both the use and abuse of power in the name of God and Torah, and often enough must decide to settle for no good at all but only for the lesser of several evils.

Normalcy and covenant, then, stand in tension where Jewish politics is concerned now as ever before in Jewish history—and both continue to stand before Jews in large part as aspiration rather than achievement. "Normalization" is not complete in either country. American Jews cleave to a unique self-definition as both religious and ethnic group and maintain a unique relationship to a sovereign state overseas. They are aware that Jewish freedom is extraordinary and their opportunities both fragile and hard-won; that the anti-Semites must be kept in mind; that the community's overarching responsibilities to the Jewish people as a whole and its enduring commitment to the covenant must always be considered. Israel for its part is hardly a nation like all others. It has existed in a near-constant state of war for almost fifty years now. What is more, the "Jewish State" acts in the name of a people who mostly live outside its borders as well as in the name of its own citizens—many of whom are not Jews. It derives legitimacy, finally, not only from the will of those it governs but from the age-old quest for Zion, site of the covenant's fulfillment.

Both Israelis and American Jews, then, in a very real sense await and depend upon the coming of messiah: Israelis because, given the normal course of power politics, the odds are heavily stacked against their state's long-term survival in the Middle East; American Jews because their vitality, if not their actual survival, depends on the achievement of a true pluralism and tolerance that until now in the world's history has been a utopian dream rather than a political reality.

That perhaps explains why the proper balance between covenant and normalcy, the theory and the practice of Jewish politics—elusive among every group, in every time and place—has been particularly difficult for Jews to locate in recent decades. But a rethinking of Jewish power and its uses has begun. I hope to further it in this chapter, through reflections about Israeli and American Jewish politics stimulated by the Book of Numbers.

The book well suits both our situation and our needs, I think. We require its reiteration of covenantal ideals as well as its many testimonies to normalcy's frustrations. I assume, in keeping with the text's own wanderings, that in political as in "religious" matters unity will continue to elude both Israelis and American Jews (though it has sometimes been forthcoming when dictated by common threat or interest). But I also believe, again following the Torah's lead, that Jewish tradition has *and must have* a great deal to say about issues of the day, and that the Torah requires (or strongly suggests) positions on these issues which depart from the policies of liberalism and conservatism, Democrats and Republicans, alike—as they depart in Israel from the platform of any party currently represented in the Knesset. The point, now more than ever, is not agreement on what Torah demands but political argument in the framework of Jewish tradition. It is a heady time for Jewish politics: a time for Jews, Torah in hand, to stand up and be counted.

Wandering toward Promise

Numbers begins with a head count—a marker at the very outset of political normalcy. God tells Moses to "raise the head of all the congregation of the children of Israel, family by family." "The idea of distributive justice presupposes a bounded world within which distribution takes place," writes Michael Walzer, "a group of people committed to dividing, exchanging, and sharing social goods, first of all among themselves. That world . . . is the political community."[3] Numbers organizes Israel tribe by tribe, assigning each a place in the small territory of the people's portable encampment. Levites, denied a normal place in the camp as they will be denied a regular inheritance in the Land, are assigned special responsibilities as well as a place alongside the Tent of Meeting, which of course stands at the very center of the camp's concentric rectangles. The census accomplished, the polity-in-formation is prepared for its marching orders. Normalcy has submitted to covenant. "Raise their heads" means "have Israel stand up to be counted, make them present and responsible before God."

We often lose sight of these opening chapters in the tumult which follows, inevitably so perhaps. The text, like its subjects, is off balance. Waywardness fast outpaces blessing. "Israel did exactly as the Lord commanded," we are told near the beginning (2:34), and are meant (knowing what follows) to read in the words, "for once!" The point at the outset is to carry over the vision of perfection given in Leviticus—to put sacred symmetry into motion, as it were—lest Numbers' subsequent and convincing portrayal of human frailty and self-destructiveness cause us to forget the human potential which we carry. God needs to exploit that potential in educating Israel, and through it the world, to a politics more noble than any yet known.

The reason not to give up on humanity is highlighted beautifully in the incantatory words of the "priestly benediction" (6:22–27). "May the Lord bless you and protect you. May the Lord cause His face to shine upon you and be gracious unto you. May the Lord lift His face up to you and grant you peace." We mistake the intent of these three blessings, I think, if we reduce them to mere expression of fond hope or read them as a wish we might all say casually or sincerely to one another, on the order of "God bless you" after a sneeze. The language is too highly charged for that, too rhythmic and formulaic. Its serial blessings are composed of three words, five words and seven words respectively in the Hebrew. The otherwise unpronounceable name of God occupies the same position in each blessing. Even the number of syllables in each verse forms a pattern.

One is therefore tempted to go to the other extreme and regard the priestly utterance as magic: an incantation pure and simple, capable of calling down God's blessing automatically via the pronunciation of God's otherwise unspeakable name. This too is a mistake, I think. The text stresses that *God* "will bless and protect you" and ends with the coda "Thus . . . *I* will bless them." The source of blessing is divine decision, not human magic.

Both misreadings miss the point the text wants to emphasize. The first (expression of fond hope) *makes Jewish politics futile* by denying human beings the power to effect significant blessing. The second (magical incantation) *makes Jewish politics unnecessary*, in that God will either bless us or will not, depending on whether the magic is effective. Each reading robs human beings of responsibility for the world even as it denies God freedom and/or efficacy. Politics in the wilderness, according to Numbers, is neither futile nor unnecessary but rather, like us, both flawed and transcendent. God is neither manipulable nor irrelevant—even if God is also not predictable.

I read the passage this way: The priests are in the text's view analogous to the Sabbath day, blessed by God at the end of the story of creation (Genesis 2:3). They are a *divinely appointed vehicle for blessing*. God's gift streams through them more efficaciously than through others. But God's favor to them is neither automatic nor exclusive. Like the blessing bestowed on all humanity in the creation story (1:28), this one too depends on what its recipients do with it. Human action and divine initiative, working in uneasy partnership, are both required if blessing is to be pronounced and accomplished.

In the first of the benedictions, God guarantees the essential conditions for human fulfillment: life and the goods necessary for life. The second blessing reminds us that it is up to us to take the reflected light of God's glory that shines from our faces—the inner light that animates and ensouls us—and bestow it upon others. Faces receive light as bodies receive food. The source is divine, the agency human. All Israel can do this, not only priests; all human beings, not only Israel. If there were no holding back, no care for the well-being ultimately in God's care, we would attain the third blessing: God's "face [would be perpetually] raised to us." God would stand with Israel, be numbered with humanity, as the Israelites "raised their heads" to be counted in the census. The wording in the Hebrew is exactly the same in both cases: a symmetry of divine and human standing opposite one another, reflecting each other's activity and light.

This truly is peace, fulfillment, want of nothing—an unattainable ideal that is the very opposite of the desire and discontent that abound in the Book of Numbers. It is a degree of blessing which—exactly like the promised land—can be known to us, if we live right, but can never actually be possessed once and for all. Jewish politics takes place in the world, not in the Garden of Eden. There is no going back to paradise. But access to the promised land, hope of it, enables one to transcend the basest practices of wilderness.

The Israelites portrayed in Numbers are not irredeemable, and certainly not evil. They are, however, frightened—and perhaps even traumatized: by slavery, by the narrow escape at the Red Sea, by the wilderness all around them, and by the terrifying uncertainty of dealing with their inscrutable Redeemer. Desire not surprisingly often gets the best of the people. Their wants are nearly endless, and as a result they frequently fail to see their situation clearly. The bodily organ which perhaps speaks loudest in the book is the stomach. "If only we had meat to eat!" the people complain at one point. "We remember the fish that we used to eat free in Egypt, the cucumbers, the melons, the leeks, the onions, and the garlic. Now our gullets are shriveled. There is nothing at all! Nothing but this manna to look at" (11:4–6). Such discontents abound. The language captures desire unfulfilled, conjuring rich images in the mind—as desire does—of what the body would like if only desire were fulfilled, and pathetically false memories of what the body had supposedly once enjoyed. Moses more than once is ready to give up: "Where am I to get meat to give all this people, when they whine before me?" (11:13).

Farce soon gives way to tragedy. God orders Moses to send men into Canaan to scout out the land. How else could they possibly conquer it? Pure normalcy here; Moses wisely selects twelve chieftains (their report must carry weight with the people), and they return with an assessment which begins with the facts but quickly gives way to distortions shaped by fear (13:27–33): "We came to see the land you sent us to; it does indeed flow with milk and honey, and this [they hold clusters of grapes] is its fruit." So far so good. They have faithfully brought back evidence, to be seen and tasted, of the land's promise. "However, the people who inhabit the country are powerful, and the cities are fortified and very large; moreover, we saw the Anakim there." This too is reasonable. They are military scouts, after all. It is their job to measure and warn of the enemy's strength. But now comes the distortion. "All the people we saw in it are of great size. . . . We looked like grasshoppers to ourselves, and so we must have looked to them." The judgment is understandable but fatal. Exaggerating the real obstacles before them, the spies have diminished themselves, the people as a whole, and God. Agents of blessing are reduced to grasshoppers. How could others not regard them in like manner? The psychological dynamics, and the workings of the political rhetoric, are both well known to us.

Moses cannot afford such a misreading of experience at this point in Israel's history. His problem is precisely that the people know only what they know—wilderness, and before that, slavery. The promise held out by God in the covenant seems only that to them: a promise, mere words, that will likely never be made good. Prophecy is one thing and politics another. Caleb's assurance that "we shall gain possession of the land," i.e., "we can do it," strains credibility. His plea that "the Lord is with us . . . have no fear then of the people of the land" likewise contravenes most known human experience, in which God's aid is, to put it mildly, undependable and erratic. The miraculous rescue at the Red Sea cannot be taken as the norm. Too much evil has transpired without God appearing to prevent it. Indeed God has at times seemed the source of evil, as when Nadav and Avihu are struck down (Leviticus 10:1–2) because they offered a sacrifice not quite according to God's instructions.

Obviously shaken by the spies' report, Moses has in his arsenal of persuasion only words and more words: reminders of divine salvations past, urgings of the unprecedented possibility vouchsafed Israel in the covenant. None of his words can stand up against the report of these twelve chieftains, ten of whom argue the case for reality—the wilderness all around them, the hunger in their bellies, crying children, their lame elders. Moses' vision is so implausible—and, if wilderness is ever to yield to promise, so urgently required.

There is a still more insurmountable obstacle to the realization of vision, however, a reality that always limits human experience and blocks human achievement, and which frequently activates fear and arouses aggression: death. "Would we had died in the land of Egypt or would we had died in this wilderness!" moan the spies (14:2). Die they will. God condemns them all to perish in their wandering. "As I live, says the Lord"—God always lives, unlike us—"I will do to you just as you have urged me. In this very wilderness shall your carcasses drop!" (14:28).

The census which began the Book of Numbers now becomes a death count. Every one of the male Israelite heads raised for battle will be lopped off somewhere in the desert, having run from battle. God's death wish for the recalcitrant people, unassuaged even by Moses' artful pleading, is as powerful as their own. The familiar designation of the "children of Israel" henceforth takes on new meaning. Only the *children* of the wilderness generation will live to see God's promise of the land fulfilled some forty years hence. Not even Moses, it later transpires, will get there. Caleb and Joshua, who saw the promise and did not doubt its attainment, are the only adults who will live to see it fulfilled in their old age.

Modern rabbis, like ancient commentators, tend to avoid the horrible implications of this passage. They point out perceptively that revolution is never easily accomplished because the total transformation of reality cannot be imagined. People inured to slavery, we are told, cannot handle freedom. Painful education is required. That may be true, but the Torah as usual is starker and more profound. It pictures God condemning an entire generation to death in a single sentence—thereby letting Moses duck responsibility for their fate in a way we would never allow to any real-world political leader.

Is it any wonder that the people rebel against this verdict and seek, on second thought, to conquer the land—only to fall back in utter defeat? It is no surprise that in the Korah story, which follows at once, the Israelites seek to blame the messenger for God's bad tidings by overthrowing Moses in favor of his near relatives in the tribe of Levi. Even after the presence of the Lord has appeared to ratify Moses' authority and the earth has swallowed the rebels and their families alive (in chapter 16), "the whole Israelite community railed against Moses and Aaron, saying, 'You two have brought death upon the Lord's people'" (17:6). This provokes yet another miraculous demonstration of Moses' authority and finally the woeful cry by the people, "Lo, we perish! We are lost, all of us lost! Everyone who so much as ventures near the Lord's tabernacle must die. Alas, we are doomed to perish!"

So they are, of course. So we all are. Death in the wilderness of Sinai takes on mythic proportions, is larger-than-life and particularly painful, because of the travail of perennial wandering and the knowledge of a tangible fulfillment that one will never live to see. But most of the normal consolations in the face of death have already been given and the Israelites must settle for them. Immediately after the story of the spies, God pointedly says, "When you enter the land that I am giving you to settle in"—the "you" clearly meaning "your children," with whom Israelite adults in the wilderness must completely identify if they hope to see fulfillment of God's promise (15:2). The point is then repeated: "When you enter the land to which I am taking you and eat of the bread of the land . . ." (15:18).

In the meantime the Levites get new duties, and the Israelites as a whole, new laws. By the close of the book, normalcy and covenant seem more in balance. The journey proceeds. Canaanite territory is assigned to the tribes. Provisions are made for inheriting it. Battles are fought and won. God is more often than not obeyed. The wilderness remains wilderness, and people still die in it every day, but it has God's presence and, more to the point, it has many of the things that make life good: love and children, work and play, the norms and ideas that provide meaning. All but the comforts of home: a time and space and bit of earth to call one's own. And that too is coming. The Israelites, then, did more than toil those many years. Like us, they danced and sang and worked and took on the mystery of things. And so the journey proceeded and proceeds.

Even so: had the Torah ended with the wilderness generation, Jewish politics and the vision of life that drives it would have been far grimmer than they are. Numbers is not the end of the Torah, let alone of the Bible. Nor does it exhaust the political models generated by Jewish historical experience. Immediately after Numbers comes Deuteronomy, in which the Israelites prepare to enter the promised land and taste fulfillment. Moses, urging them and us on to achievement, provides a grand vision of human possibility that, he hopes, will not remain with him on the far side of the Jordan. His words are meant to counter with reasonable hope the people's inevitable failure and disappointment. Israel *does* enter the land, under Joshua, and conquers it. The historical and prophetic writings show the people conducting themselves over the centuries of sovereignty neither as saints dutifully obeying every divine command, nor as rogues flouting every command with disregard and impunity. If the texts are at all true to the facts of actual history, the situation of the covenant, like the people charged with putting it into practice, was neither all good nor all bad. Prophets did not demand perfection but justice and, failing that, repentance. Sin and virtue coexisted. There was punishment, but also return.

After the destruction of the Second Temple by the Romans in 70 C.E.—a punishment foreshadowing no return until the Messiah—the rabbis assumed the mantle of leadership once held by priests and prophets and extended many of the disciplines formerly aimed at priestly holiness to all Jews in every country of the dispersion. The task of Jewish politics changed from the ordering of a sacred commonwealth in the promised land to the construction and maintenance of Jewish communities in far-flung exile. Torah, interpreted in countless commentaries, became the constitution of a cultural and political minority which was constantly subject to Gentile laws beyond its sway. The rabbis could promise no divine miracles to defeat Israel's enemies in the short term and could perform none to validate their own authority. God would not appear to swallow up latter-day Korahs or cause the staffs of latter-day Aarons to blossom as proof of their just rule. Jews would have to make their way politically through other, more normal means, cleaving to (and where necessary compromising) observance of the covenant as they went. "The law of the land," they recognized, "is the law." History, meaning God, had determined this.

Arguably, however, the political relevance of the Torah, and particularly of Numbers, was abiding. For Israel was in exile, and the fundamentals of the human condition had not changed with the centuries. Wilderness—like everything else in Torah—took on new meanings. The perpetuation of Jewish sacred order during the people's millennial wanderings depended upon the provision of a life meaningful and rich enough to secure Jewish allegiance despite the inevitable tendencies of a weak and often persecuted people to despair and dissolution.

That task was facilitated, but could not be guaranteed, by the degree of legal autonomy provided to every Jewish community by the Gentile rulers to whom they were ultimately subject. Communal coercion and the lack of a realistic alternative identity no doubt helped to keep Jews Jewish over the centuries. However, they could not have sufficed to make that existence heavy with meaning, as it apparently was—for here we are today to tell the tale. To do that the conviction of continuity with the Torah was required, along with the hope of messianic fulfillment. Jews had to believe in their dispersion that they were still following Moses through the wilderness, and looking as he had toward (return to) the promised land.

Rabbinic norms and expectations shaped Jewish politics (in concert with forces over which Jews had no control) until the transformation of modernity described in the opening chapters of this essay. Emancipation and Zionism have greatly altered the nature and the extent of the power that Jews wield. They have also significantly changed the kinds of communities that Jews can seek to maintain or imagine. The Jewish situation in America and in Israel today is less like the wilderness pictured in Numbers than ever before. In neither place do Jews any longer live in exile. They enjoy an unprecedented degree of normalcy in both countries, and in response to new conditions have substantially altered (when not actually abandoning) the covenant.

But—the most decisive consideration, in my view—the "human-all-too-human" basics of politics in the world we have not fundamentally changed. The messiah has not come. Jews still have not reached the promised land, even in Israel. Numbers therefore remains highly relevant to both the theory and the practice of Jewish politics in our day. Several features of its vision seem to me particularly enduring.

The first is the *need for law*. Human beings, complex mixtures of drives to good and evil, require direction and restraint if they are to know the good and do it. This was Reinhold Niebuhr's potent message in *Moral Man and Immoral Society* (1932). It was folly, he argued, to believe that "the egoism of individuals is being progressively checked by the development of rationality or the growth of a religiously inspired goodwill and that nothing but the continuance of this process is necessary to establish social harmony between all the human societies and collectives." There was also sin to reckon with. Moral progress will always be uncertain.[4]

Nor is *experience* always positive, or to be trusted. It requires ample room for growth and change, but also needs limits and a framework of interpretation. One should not go "exploring after eyes and heart" (15:39), we are told at the conclusion of the narrative about the spies. The Hebrew explicitly calls to mind the charge to the explorers of Canaan with which the episode began. For "reality" is always open to multiple interpretations, and perception can fall victim to self-deception. Desire can and does lead one astray. Hence the need for reminders, such as the fringes on Israelite garments, that it is not good to see or do everything. Jewish politics can never proclaim, as Korah did in effect, "just trust the people. We are all holy, after all." The Torah does trust people—and, because people are not perfect, mistrusts them as well. Jews are and will remain, as Philip Rieff once put it, a law-and-order people.[5]

Second, however, Jewish tradition is also keenly aware that law and order are means, not end. *The point is to have justice. The goal is not order but Torah.* And the existence of the covenant, from the Torah's point of view, provides the guarantee that human beings are worthy to receive it. That is why politics is not for Jews a completely tragic pursuit. Much good can be done. Progress can be made. Human beings are created in the image of God, after all, capable of receiving and initiating blessing. The combination of reason, tradition, and experience confers ample knowledge of the good. Humanity's array of religious and cultural traditions over the centuries, despite the obvious differences among them, have agreed to a remarkable extent about the proper moral direction. These resources are particularly critical today, when prophecy is long gone from Jewish life (the rabbis decreed it a thing of the past two thousand years ago), the authority of holy men arouses suspicion far more than obedience (at least outside the Orthodox world), and most Jews feel accountable to some norms at least that do not originate in Torah alone.

The rabbis opened the way to cooperation with non-Jews in discerning and pursuing the good by dividing the world not into two categories—Jews and Gentiles—but into three: Jews, "children of Noah," and idolaters. Pluralism is built into this conception. Multiculturalism of a sort is not only presumed but valued. Jews are those obligated by Torah. "Children of Noah" (though variously defined across the centuries) share the most essential principles of belief and conduct with Jews. They too are partners to a divine covenant and, while retaining their differing identities, are (if moral) counted righteous and apportioned a "share in the world to come." Idolaters stand for truths Jews hold false and, more importantly, engage in practices Jews hold pernicious. They must therefore be opposed. In the modern world, rabbinic authorities agree, we cannot identify the last category with any existing nation or religion but only with evil individuals or with nations temporarily bent (like Nazi Germany) to an evil will. Even were there no idolaters on earth, but only Jews and children of Noah, we would still be unable to end conflict and secure peace and goodwill. Sin is eternal. We all bear God's image but remain mortal—and therefore in need of mutual cooperation and correction.

Obedience to Torah and fidelity to covenant imply the relativization of all other loyalties—political loyalties first among them. One must speak carefully here, lest anti-Semites seize upon the truth—that Jews according to the terms of covenant owe ultimate allegiance to God and the good—in order to declaim the falsehood that Jews therefore cannot be loyal to their country. That is nonsense. Experience has proven it so. Dual loyalties is an accusation without foundation where American Jewry is concerned. What is more, the latent conflict between patriotism and moral duty is hardly unique to Jews. It has been a feature of Western discourse at least since Sophocles' *Antigone*. But one should not, out of fear of the distortion, avoid facing up to the truth: the Torah's insistence that politics always be *means* and never *end*.

Indeed, the text views power as notoriously unstable and easily swayed. Joseph's ups and downs in Egypt are the first in a long series of tales which make the point that the fate of Jews (and others) too often depends upon whim, desire, and good fortune. Esther's rescue of her people from Haman is another case in point. Jewish history ancient and modern abounds in such cases. A Roman emperor goes mad, and devastation follows. A czar is assassinated, and the course of Jewish history changes. The Israeli prime minister is assassinated, and the course of Israeli history changes. One day Gorbachev is in power, the next day he is not, then he is again, and again is not. The good and bad of these ups and downs will not be calculable for years to come, if ever. Normalcy by definition is as relative as circumstance, ever adapting to conditions on the ground. The end, always covenant, abides.

All of this, finally, makes for an *attitude of sober realism toward politics,* particularly when it comes to the possibilities of good and evil stored up in power. We do the best we can with what we have, guided ideally by the wisest we know. Jewish politics have historically been cautious—not only because a small minority must be watchful if it is to survive in the world and protect its interests, but because human imagination and achievement of the good, as the Torah sees it, can be extended only incrementally. Zionists used to mock this caution. Indeed many Israelis still maintain that Jews for two millennia exercised no power whatever and therefore stood "outside history," as if only sovereign states have agency and only "manly" struts upon the world's stage should be counted as power.[6] The rabbis knew better. Jews *walk* through the wilderness, as in Numbers, and do so as it were one step at a time. Leaping too far, like the Israelites bent on immediate conquest of the Land, or messianists attempting to "force the end" of history before God or humanity is prepared, we overreach ourselves and get lost. Absolutes have proven dangerous to Jews time and again, except as promises one strives to keep, clouds of smoke and pillars of fire that guide one fitfully.

There are no Jewish shortcuts to the promised lands of peace and justice—all the more reason for the *hope* required to sustain one in the meantime. Some days it seems we might as well give up. The sense of helplessness surrounds us as surely as the wilderness. I am writing on such a day, when the peace process in the Middle East seems stalled yet again to the point of extinction. Numbers has prepared us for such moments, I believe. It arms us with the knowledge that it may take a long time to reach even small fulfillments, and nonetheless urges the conviction that the goal really is there to pursue, and can be pursued with some success.

The text positively shouts this at us at the end of Numbers and the start of Deuteronomy. You *will* get there. You *can* get it right. And if you don't, your children will. God has not set you up for eternal failure. In the rabbis' terms, expressed in Pirke Avot: the labor is worthwhile and you must begin it, even if you yourself cannot complete it. You've got to believe, for all that life breaks your heart, that you can go on—and actually get somewhere worthwhile.

Israel: The Quest for Covenantal Normalcy

There is a well-known joke in Israel which my wife and I heard often when we arrived in 1984 with the intention of settling permanently. It is about the day when David Ben Gurion, the country's first prime minister, arrived in the afterworld and was given a choice between the two locations in which eternity can be passed. "Let me visit them before I decide," he requests, and he is promptly shown a heavenly salon full of boring conversations among pious old men, insipid music droning in the background. The other place is lush with fine violins, delicious food, and beautiful young women. He returns to the gateway and without hesitation chooses hell—only to discover, when he returns to take up residence, that it has been transformed into fire and brimstone, torment unending. "It looks so different now!" Ben Gurion exclaims. "Ah," says the guide. "Before you were a tourist. Now you are a new immigrant!"

The Book of Numbers—and recent events in Israel—suggest another meaning for that joke, far more despondent in its reference than

the plight of individual immigrants confronting the formidable bu-
reaucracies of the Interior Ministry and the Jewish Agency (which in
our case, by the way, performed quite well). In this reading Israel itself
is the new immigrant, the *oleh hadash,* which has recently "ascended" to the blessings and curses of statehood. The power that
looked so welcoming when it beckoned from a distance is now
regarded even by those who hold it with some ambivalence. It is one
thing to *explore* the uses of sovereignty for the first time (the modern
Hebrew word for "tourist" in the joke is derived from the biblical
root that sent the spies on their expedition into Canaan). One can do
so much good: provide refuge to the homeless, save Jews from
persecution, initiate new arrangements for collective living, make the
desert bloom, pursue justice in fact and not just in principle. But it is
quite another thing to learn the hard way that power is often not
sufficient to accomplish the good for which its use is intended, that
one does much evil with it while pursuing good, and that power
exercised wrongly actually diminishes those who wield it.

I intend no preachment here, but only a statement of facts always
more obvious in retrospect. Nor do I hold any brief for powerlessness. The normalcy of Jewish statehood is infinitely preferable to the
inability of Jews in exile over the centuries to defend themselves.
Covenant is not well served by powerlessness. Neither is virtue. But
the costs of power, the damage done to covenant by power, should
also not be denied. They comprise the burden of Jewish politics in
our day.

Some American Jews—though far fewer than several years ago—
would argue that I, as an American Jew, can have nothing legitimate
to say on the subject of Israeli foreign and domestic policy. Israeli
soldiers do the fighting, Israeli lives are exposed to terrorism daily;
how dare I publicly discuss their situation from the comfort of my
home in Palo Alto? When my wife and I decided to return to America
in 1986, according to this view, I forfeited my right to criticize Israeli
policy. And, the argument continues, Israel gets such negative public-
ity in U.S. media as it is! Why make its image even worse by criticizing
it from afar, thereby aiding and abetting the anti-Semites whose
reason for attacking the Jewish State is clear, and encouraging
American policymakers to weaken the support on which Israel's
existence depends?

These arguments are not wholly without merit, to my mind. There is substantial media bias against Israel, and those who bear the risks should of course have the leading voice. But the merits of silence are far outweighed by three considerations.

One: all Jews have a stake in this debate, wherever they live. The Jewish State acts in the name of world Jewry, appeals to its tradition, invokes its God. American Jewish opponents of Rabin's policies, many of whom had denounced expressions of support by American Jews for those policies when Yitzhak Shamir was prime minister, proved vociferous in condemning them once Rabin took power. They had every right to speak up, I believe, as do I.

Two: I have seen no evidence that Israel has been harmed by responsible American Jewish criticism, quite the opposite. American aid for Israel, a major item in our national budget, let alone Israel's, depends upon the support of credible Jewish spokesmen who do more than parrot Israeli government policy. Prudence has always been a mark of diaspora politics, and rightfully so, for it marks political maturity. The need now too is for caution, not for silence.

Three: both the Zionist claim to "normalization," to being a nation like all other nations, and the American Jewish claim to being fully at home in this country, a place where Jews finally have as much right as anyone to speak their minds and pursue their interests, are contradicted if Jews keep their mouths shut about issues of paramount concern to them and of major import to all Americans. At the moment Jewish politics in both Israel and the diaspora demands critical political theory and impassioned political argument, not least when it comes to the single most important item on the Jewish political agenda in our time—Israel's conflict with the Palestinians. For that is also the single greatest moral challenge confronting contemporary Jews, yet another reason that the argument for silence is not persuasive.

I see no need to spell out my position on the substance of the Middle East conflict in any detail. Jews have been engaged in this quarrel for nearly three decades now. More important, the Rabin-Peres government articulated the views I would advocate eloquently on many occasions and began to put them into practice in a manner that, until the summer of 1996, seemed irreversible. Their policy was a graphic example of the synthesis between normalcy and covenant—and of the tension which inevitably besets such syntheses. It was clear from the outset, for example, that the territorial compromise at the heart of their policy would not be risk-free. Rabin and Peres wagered, however—as would I, following the informed opinion of the generals—that the considerable military risk of ceding significant portions of the West Bank to Palestinian control is preferable to the danger to life and property posed to Israel by holding over a million Palestinians inside Israel's borders against their will. It is preferable to the political danger posed to Israeli democracy by permanent subjugation of that population without granting it equal rights of citizenship. And it is preferable to the consequent demographic danger to Israel's Jewish majority and hence its status as a Jewish state. If Israel wishes to be a Jewish democracy, Rabin concluded, it has no choice but to reach a compromise with the Palestinians that involves giving up control over Palestinian population centers—and so of substantial portions of the biblical land of Israel.

"Peace Now," as I understand the movement which had long advocated such compromise, and which sponsored the rally at which Rabin was assassinated, does not deny the many obstacles to peace on both sides of the battle lines or believe that a settlement will mean mutual love and affection between Arabs and Jews. Certainly the Israeli backers of Peace Now whom I know do not believe that peace in the sense of full mutual acceptance is possible now or any time soon. The movement was founded in 1978 by reserve officers, pragmatists by training; the point of the movement's name is not to proclaim the arrival of utopia but to emphasize that every day Israel—like its opponents—either takes steps toward peace or away from it. Jews cannot force Palestinians or Arab states to move toward peace but they can incline them in the opposite direction and can move toward peace themselves. Right-wing rhetoric has consistently sought to portray this stance as naive at best, at worst unpatriotic and fatal to Israel's security. "How can you trust the Arabs to keep agreements?" they ask. To which I reply, echoing the Labor government: my trust is not in the other side's promises but in the ability of Israel's defense forces. That ability to protect the State has not been and must not be surrendered.

I myself have little confidence that anything like real peace is at hand. Tragedy haunts all politics, and none more so than the modern political history of the Jews, who have been searching over the past two centuries for a place where they can exist on this earth securely. The Holocaust and countless other persecutions demonstrate how futile that search has often been. In central and eastern Europe the Jewish people was nearly eradicated. Its "secure refuge" in Zion remains under siege. Jews have achieved a measure of security, for the time being at least, in only a handful of diaspora nations in the West—always with significant compromise of their distinctiveness. Any Jew alert to these facts (and attuned to the Book of Numbers!) is not likely to believe that people make peace with others because they are inherently rational or good-hearted or inclined by nature to live and let live. It is true that *inside* the various national borders of the world, the rule of law and not of force holds sway. But force often hides just out of view and law can give way quickly to mob violence, as it has in America's urban riots in recent decades. *Across* borders the law of the jungle is still barely restrained, particularly where hatred and conflict have long prevailed.

In Israel the tragedy which haunts all politics is ever in full view. Many Palestinians press their claims daily to the entirety of the Land of Israel—not just the West Bank or East Jerusalem—and do so before the eyes of the world's cameras as well as in the faces of the Jews who pass them on the street. One cannot look away. Others are prepared for tactical reasons to settle for part of the land, in the hope that in the long run the Jews will disappear from it just as the Crusaders did a thousand years ago. Arab opponents of Israel are not about to reconcile themselves to the existence of a Jewish State in the midst of "Arab territory." A love powerful enough to overcome decades of bitter strife is not about to break out in the city of Jerusalem. "Messiah has not come," a popular Israeli rock song put it a few years back. "He hasn't even telephoned."

Hence the enormous temptation to view events as tragedies which all are helpless to deter and to step back from politics into private contentments—or, worse, to join forces with "the inevitable" by letting conflict take its natural course, a spiral downward. Hence too the importance of recalling the lessons of the wilderness. The need is for a politics of sober realism which says, Nevertheless, there are choices to be made, there are accommodations which can be reached and trust which can be extended. In the short term—the only term for which politics is suited—one can be persuaded by mutual interest and exhaustion of other alternatives to live and let live rather than kill and be killed. Now as always, it is wise to be cautious but forbidden not to hope.

The standard which should guide and judge covenantal Jewish politics in making any compromise for peace cannot be messianic or prophetic or in any sense absolute. Both normalcy and covenant must be served. We should refuse on the one hand to judge Jews by different and higher criteria than any other people, especially when existence is at stake. Jews need not be guiltless of all injustice and innocent of any crime in order for their acquisition of the land of Israel to be counted (relatively, as always) just and their claim to the land to be valid. On the other hand we should not exonerate Israel of responsibility for the evil it commits just because its very existence is at stake. Jews will always demand more of Israel than they do of other nations, because that is the nature of Jews and Torah. Jewish history and tradition make us so. Israel is the Jewish State, and as such is subject to the high ideals which have ennobled Jewish (and human) life for many centuries now. Jews would not be Jews, recognizable to themselves and others as such, were high moral demand not a distinguishing element of the way they talk to each other and conduct their politics. Nor would Israel inspire Jews (and many Gentiles) if it did not subscribe to the highest human and Jewish ideals of our time—and to a significant degree live up to them.

But Jews are also a people like any other, returned since 1948 to majority rule of a state among states. Our standard in judging Israel should therefore not be unique. In weighing the risks that Israel should undertake in the name of compromise, we need criteria that occupy middle ground between absolutist demands for prophetic righteousness on one side, and, on the other, realpolitik arguments that Israel must play by the same laws of the jungle that govern the foreign policy of most other states, and must act all the more brutally because it does not have the room for error enjoyed by greater powers.

Buber, I think, came closest to formulating that middle ground (though I disagree strongly with his call for a binational state rather than a multicultural state with a Jewish majority). "In every hour of decision we [must be] aware of our responsibility and summon our conscience to weigh exactly how much [force or injustice] is necessary to preserve the community, and accept just so much and no more."[7] His standard seems to me directly applicable to both the moral and political complexities of Israel's present situation.

It reminds us, first of all, that *politics begins with force.* "Politics for us," Max Weber wrote, "means striving to share power or striving to influence the distribution of power, either among states or among groups within a state. . . . 'Every state is founded on force,' said Trotsky at Brest-Litovsk. That is indeed right."[8] For Jews, who were relatively powerless for two millennia, the ability to deploy power in one's own defense comes as an incalculable gift, a blessing that far outweighs the accompanying curses. It remains essential on a daily basis to Jewish survival. The enemies Israel faces are real. The danger facing it is clear and present. If those who have a competing claim to the Land will not let Jews live, the state will defend itself—with full support of the standard Buber enunciated. Jewish politics is determinedly pragmatic rather than utopian. It is made for the world's normal wilderness, which now, thanks to Zionism, has come to include the "promised land."

Note too that Buber provides for *disagreement among people of goodwill about what is necessary to ensure survival.* He is aware of the obvious difficulty in calibrating the precise degree of force required for that end, particularly in the heat of battle. Those who immediately condemn any apparent excess fail to uphold the rigors of this standard. So do messianists bent on retaining the West Bank no matter what the cost in human suffering, on grounds that God gave Jews this land or that their ancestors walked it. Those who justify any use of power in their own behalf, no matter how excessive, fail to make careful calculations of the sort Buber stipulated—and so abandon the balanced Jewish politics which, though covenantal, always remains an art of the possible.

I understand the West Bank settler who addresses the Land in beautiful Hebrew, telling "her" that "we have returned to you, you who have lain waste for centuries; we have not forgotten you, and will never leave you again." The author is stirred by prophetic passages that I too hold dear. I love the land, uncannily so for a person raised so far away. I appreciate what it means for Jews and for Torah that Jews have returned to it. But the injustice sanctioned by the settler's poetic appeal is considerable. So is the blindness it encourages to the real human beings living unnoticed right in front of the speaker's face. I much prefer the mangled Hebrew of the generals, their speech overflowing with military acronyms as they pragmatically calculate the risks worth taking in the name of defense. The newspaper lexicon of terms for unemployment, recession, industry, and environmental protection is also preferable—first fruits of Jewish normalcy, the news not in wartime or on Sabbaths but on weekdays. Reasoned prose on both sides of the argument, even bad prose, serves normal politics better than inspirational verse tending toward apocalypse.

If the generals agreed that Israel's security would be threatened militarily by giving up control of population centers on the West Bank, I would urge another solution to the problem in the name of justice than territorial compromise, and Rabin would have done so long before me. But the facts seem quite the opposite. Whereas strategic depth of the sort gained in the agreement with Egypt that demilitarized the Sinai is essential to Israeli security, control of Nablus and Hebron is not, and may actually be a liability. The settlers living there do not assist the state's security. They are there to make and enforce biblical claims, messianic claims. But Jews are possessed of a tradition which always insists on realism in politics rather than utopia. If the military strategists (Rabin first among them) have concluded that from Israel's side there *is* an alternative to war and repression in defense of "Greater Israel," Israel seems to me compelled to adopt Buber's standard: no more force or injustice than is absolutely necessary.

Covenant as well as normalcy demands this. Israel will not be a Jewish State if Jews compose only a minority of its citizens. Neither will it be a Jewish State if that minority imposes its will by force on a majority who are denied equal citizenship, or if the minority develops Jewish culture and religion at the expense of another people or of other traditions kept in forcible submission. Like Buber, I cannot countenance the idea that the Jewish people waited two thousand years for restoration of its sovereignty, for the renewed opportunity to put Judaism into practice in a Jewish polity, economy, and society instead of within the "four ells of halakhah," just to found a repressive antidemocratic state that discriminates against non-Jews and practices political business as usual according to standards no higher than the usual. The covenant must have its voice—or rather its voices. Orthodox (much less messianist) voices cannot be allowed a monopoly on the definition of what "politics according to the covenant" should mean. Indeed Orthodox voices have for the most part been shamefully silent on issues of social justice about which the Torah has much to say.

The Jewish State is Jewish in a serious covenantal sense only insofar as it (1) works to implement the prophetic and rabbinic call for social justice in all areas of social, political, and economic life, within the generous limits of the possible, and (2) provides the arena in which competing definitions of Jewish tradition and Jewish community coexist with each other (and with non-Jewish cultures) as they struggle democratically for the allegiance of Jewish souls and the shaping of a Jewish society (in which non-Jews and their visions are strongly represented). Israel can justly claim the legitimation of Judaism only insofar as its Jewish citizens remain committed, regardless of how they interpret God's Torah, to the building of a just Jewish community—just, that is, to Jews and non-Jews alike, with full recognition of the variety of interpretation that will always be given to what *Jewish* community means.

This and no more: no surrender of territory that results in the loss of security; no demand for a utopian peace of love and friendship with Israel's neighbors; no hinging of Israel's right to be on the attainment or approximation of perfection. The premise of normal covenantal politics, as opposed to the absolutist politics of messianists, is that treaties between states do not signify love and trust but rather the promise to pursue advantage by peaceful means while keeping watch on the other side to make sure that it does the same. The force needed to protect the Jewish state and Jewish lives will always be permitted and demanded by the texts of Judaism, even as those same texts will deny Jews the right to fulfill the perennial desire for a larger share of scarce resources such as land, water, fields, jobs, or housing, at the expense of others.

Once again, the relevant book of the Torah is not Exodus or Leviticus but Numbers. And when abuse of covenantal prerogatives comes in the Book of Numbers, whether in the name of the "holy" Jewish people or the name of God, the Torah is unsparing in its condemnation. Israel's existence was threatened in the wilderness too, and that threat did not excuse grave wrongdoing. Nor did the wrongs committed then, if held to the minimum and atoned for, take away the people's right to live or its potential to become, under the covenant, a source of blessing.

Numbers points, finally, to a further requirement of Israeli Jewish politics in our day: *imagination*. Among Israeli leaders in recent decades, only Shimon Peres has offered a comprehensive conception of Israel's role in the Middle East, with requisite attention to the role of the Arab minority inside the Jewish State. The immense possibilities of a truly multicultural society at the crossroads of three religions and three continents have barely been limned, let alone explored. Still less has been said on matters of policy, whether foreign or domestic, in the name of Judaism—except by those who lay absolutist claim to the Land and deny non-Jews equal voice in determining Israel's future. The failure of Jewish imagination has been considerable. You can't get through any wilderness, the Torah advises, even after forty (or fifty) years, without a notion of the promised land to which you are bound. Cloud and fire must show the way: the hope of more than you are used to, clear evidence of more than the past could have led you to expect.

A New Agenda for Jewish Politics in America

American Jews tend to think (and act) as if Jewish politics is merely an Israeli concern. Church and state (so goes the argument) must remain separated in this country. Jews constitute a tiny minority of the American population. They cannot agree with one another on what the Torah wants from them. It would therefore be wrong, fatuous, and probably hopeless to try to transform the society, polity, and economy of the United States in accordance with the perceived demands of covenant. Normalcy counsels another course, the one by and large followed by the Jewish community: protection of undeniable communal interests; advocacy on behalf of Israel; personal achievement and philanthropy inside the givens of the current order; association as individuals with causes bent on gradual reform.

Once again, I see some merit in these objections to the exercise in which I am about to engage. In fact, I remember challenging Abraham Heschel with similar arguments when I met him in his office (my only extended conversation with Heschel) in 1970. With youthful arrogance I demanded to know what gave him the right to pronounce the Vietnam War a moral atrocity when the president of the United States, who knew far more about the facts, had decided the war was necessary. Many American Jews, supporters and opponents of the war alike, had looked askance at Heschel's leadership role in anti-war efforts. The former saw his activism as a case of *chutzpah*, pure and simple, while the latter worried that he would provide anti-Semites with ammunition for years to come.

In response to my doubts Heschel invoked his responsibility as a teacher of Jewish tradition not to remain silent. He explained to me that Judaism holds it a "profanation of God's name" when things are done in God's name that must never be done, according to God's Torah, and Jews are silent. It is a "sanctification of God's name" when Gentiles are led to praise Judaism and Judaism's God because of the righteousness Jews stand for and perform. Heschel reminded me that silence and aloofness are not traits that Jews have ever particularly valued. The most important religious issue of our time, he said pointedly, was not the number of kosher butchers in Philadelphia (my hometown). It was to end the Vietnam War.

I do not mean to imply, in reporting this, that Heschel (much less I) had the only "Torah-true" position on difficult issues of the day. One could (and Jews did) formulate powerful Jewish positions in support of the war. My point is that we dare not avoid such positions for fear of anti-Semitism, nor should we do so out of genuine humility before the enormity of our tradition and the complexities of the dilemmas we face. Jewish *normalcy* demands involvement in the larger societal issues of America because Jews will not be able to survive and thrive in this country if certain social, economic, and political conditions are not in place. (True pluralism and genuine multiculturalism are, for example, absolute requirements.) *Covenant,* moreover, requires as Heschel taught that the teachings of Torah be heard to speak to issues of the day—lest Jews and non-Jews come to presume the Torah's irrelevance. Jewish silence on controversial matters has done incalculable damage to the standing of the tradition in the eyes of young Jews who—if they saw Judaism at the forefront of battles which need fighting—might well not have kept their distance.

They will certainly not be brought near by a Jewish politics which is merely a copycat version (and generally watered-down at that) of either liberalism or conservatism. The former has too often been the case in this country. Why bother being Jewish? One already votes Democratic. Aren't Jewish values such as freedom and justice universal? Shouldn't liberalism then suffice? The answer—negative—must be uncompromising. At times Jewish interests and principles overlap existing positions, or combine them. In other respects, however, they provoke a stance very different from anything the major parties have yet formulated—and almost always supply a different rationale.

Liberals, for example, too often lack the Torah's tragic sense of limits. They trust too much in rational solutions to intractable problems. They too often seem ready to sacrifice particular traditions or communities in the name of abstract universal goods. Conservatives, when they invoke tradition, seem to have in mind a past that had no room for Jews and so cannot attract them now. When conservatives picture human beings as autonomous agents who come together only for specific purposes in limited associations, but otherwise seek above all else to protect individual liberties and privacy, they deny the fundamental truth of Jewish politics and Jewish history: that we are bound to each other in communities. Only through them, like it or not, will we find fulfillment.

Jewish politics, then, partakes of both positions and of neither (and thus, if the polls are correct, resembles the politics of many other Americans).[9] I want to outline the middle ground that I think Jewish politics in this country should occupy, by briefly and in general terms taking up a variety of issues high on the American political agenda in recent years. I do so to stimulate rather than to foreclose conversation; to offer example rather than proof. Other positions arising out of the "sources of Judaism" have been and will be forthcoming. That is all to the good. My aim is not to have Jews in this country speak with one voice about any issue but to have us bring the tradition to bear on as many issues as possible, in as many voices as are needed.

CULTURE

Issues of "culture" were less pronounced in the 1996 election cycle than they were in 1992, but I begin with them nonetheless because they get at the disenchantment a Jew like myself feels with liberalism and conservatism alike. Jews and Judaism of whatever sort, it seems fair to say, have a strong vested interest in *a set of orientations to tradition and authority* that have for good reasons or bad become identified in America in recent decades with conservatism. Authority is in principle not a bad thing in my eyes but rather a necessity and a good. It arouses my suspicion but also my respect. Conversely, blind faith in either "human decency" or "progress through enlightenment" seems to me misplaced. We will always need the guidance of authority—parents, teachers, leaders, sages if we can find them—to protect us from the worst in ourselves and elicit the best of which we are capable. We will need to call upon experience as much as expertise. Local wisdom may well count for more than abstract knowledge. Tradition and precedent, while hardly infallible and always in need of scrutiny and correction, should be trusted in the first instance rather than cast aside in the name of freedom or the future.

As a Jew I treasure freedom, have more than one holiday dedicated to its virtues, but also recognize all sorts of obligations to my Creator and my fellow human creatures. Every form of Judaism I know, including Reform and Reconstructionism, speaks the *language of obligation* along with that of freedom. I value autonomy as much as the next person, and detest coercion. But I also know that we must not be permitted to "do our own thing" or to "let it all hang out." A society in which "anything goes" is one in which not much good will be accomplished. "Feed the poor? How boring! House the homeless? Sure, if that's your thing; me, I'm into conspicuous consumption." I exaggerate, of course, but from where I sit in the heart of yuppiedom, not by all that much.

A Jew cannot endorse the equality of all urges. We have learned from bitter experience that the effect of undermining one authority after another, as we in America are wont to do of late, will not result in greater freedom for ourselves but in greater sway for individuals, movements, and corporations who know what they want and single-mindedly pursue it. When *those* people try to exercise power openly and without restraint, we had better have authority available to hold them in check. If not, we'll be left only with the rule of interest and brute force. Untrammeled liberalism inevitably plots its own demise.

But so does unalloyed conservatism, whether of the individualist or the traditionalist variety. I cannot as a Jew, blessed with freedoms and opportunities in the West during the past two centuries as never before, condemn modernity as some aberration from a right road last walked in the middle ages. Nor can I attack postmodernism, with its respect for minority traditions, as a steep decline from the golden fifties. I cannot view culture as an elite preserve, a gentlemen's club, from which the riffraff are excluded lest the straight and narrow be obscured. Again: I am a Jew, after all. I don't long nostalgically for the days when high culture either had no room for my people or condemned us to inferior status. I know that any culture defined exclusively by a majority will marginalize and exclude me the way that gentlemen's clubs and country clubs did for decades.

How then can I generate enthusiasm for a core curriculum that has no room in it for Jews—or women, or blacks? How can I not treasure the opportunities opened to me by modernity, the breathing room Jews have gained thanks to pluralism? Shall I leave the definition of my culture to T. S. Eliot, no friend of the Jews, or leave the "traditional canon" of Western culture in place with all its exclusions intact? I will not—any more than I will back opposition in principle to all canons. The Torah, a canon if ever there was one, is the very center of my life. You can't tell me that no books are more important than others, no teachings more right than others. I stood with neither left nor right in the curriculum debates of the eighties, cheering on the forces of the center.

As a Jew I want and need vital traditions (in the plural), just as I require and desire strong communities. I want to see traditions and communities coexisting, competing, in tension with and borrowing from one another. I also want innovation and autonomy—and want these directed, challenged, checked, by a past that we cannot dismiss and a higher authority which we cannot easily slough off. The balance will not be easy to find, of course, but it seems eminently worth seeking.

SOCIETY

The very same dissatisfaction with left and right holds, for the same reasons, when we turn from the cultural to the social issues so prominent in recent campaigns, though this time the political Jew in me tilts left rather than right. Jewish politics as I would have it pursued is *culturally conservative but socially liberal.* I mean that in the following sense. Conservatives generally seem to link a traditionalist view of culture—unitary, elitist, normative—to an individualist vision of society. They start with autonomous individual agents, as if we all sign the Enlightenment social contract again every day and thereby exit from "nature" in order to cooperate for limited purposes in specific associations. Government is suspect in that view, or even evil. Better then to leave individuals—even individual corporations—alone. The very same conservatives, however, are prepared to restrict the right to have abortions and to censor art exhibitions—even as they turn around again and declare government regulation of manufacturers unwarranted interference and see no obligation to feed the hungry unless they (or their parents) work. The Jew in me pronounces them wrong on both counts.

Jewish commitment of whatever sort begins with the command to take care of other people's bodies, and only then permits us to proceed with the improvement of our own souls. The reverse path is mistaken. Recall the talmudic discussion about gates and porters lodges in the previous chapter. No social arrangement, however worthwhile, can be permitted to prevent the cries of the poor from being heard. I am reminded of this first principle of Jewish politics every time I visit leisure complexes surrounded by walls and secured by guards who I am sure would never permit a poor person to get inside. The rabbis arranged the Jewish liturgical calendar so that no Yom Kippur ever passes without Jews reading, in the midst of their fasting and atonement, that God does not want their fast alone but rather wants them to "share bread with the hungry . . . when you see the naked, clothe him, and do not ignore your own kin."

This is basic stuff to Judaism, inculcated in me since childhood. The poor are our "own kin." There is no excluding them. They eat only if we feed them. Many American Jews have been raised on these imperatives and almost all are proud of them, even if few Jews, as few Gentiles, actually carry them out most of the time.

One can of course disagree about which welfare policy best ensures that the poor will be housed and fed. The Torah offers no brief for the platform of either major party. Neither the prophets nor the rabbis calculated the acceptable poverty level or mandated a specific distribution of the wealth. Their concern was that no one be hungry or homeless and that everyone be provided with basic human needs so that they could pursue a good life in accordance with Torah. But no traditional Jewish ethic can sanction unbridled individualism: greed made virtuous, the self glorified, the drive to consumption freely indulged. The rabbis did not conceive society as a collection of individuals bonded together by self-interest and coercion but as a federation of integral communities. The self not part of such communities would in their view be stunted and unhappy. It would do more wrong than it should, and not enough right.

America on this Jewish view is and should be held together by more than a common system of government and a shared popular culture. Our nation is founded on a vision—freedom, equality, opportunity, diversity—underwritten, as the Pledge of Allegiance reminds us, by God. The country's legitimacy is also underwritten, as the Torah would want it to be, by the way its least powerful citizens (children, the poor, the elderly) are treated and by the spiritual richness of the lives that it makes possible. If the country's founding vision is repeatedly mocked, the bonds which hold its people together are weakened, just as God's providence is mocked when the aged are cast aside: a major problem in American society. Ironically, some of the politicians most insistent on retaining the Pledge in the schools seem least committed to proving that its words "indivisible" and "for all" are still operative. Jews are driven to pursue that allegiance by interest and principle alike. Normalcy and covenant both depend on it.

The limited framework of this essay does not permit detailed consideration of any of the issues which dominate the contemporary American political agenda. There is still less room here for reasoned Jewish arguments from the sources for the particular stances which I would advocate. Again, however, my point is not to make those arguments, but to urge that we bring Torah to bear when we do so. Our tradition has much to say on issues such as abortion, censorship in the arts, the content of popular culture, family values, the ethics of health care, and the new global politics needed to safeguard the planet's resources. No less important, the Torah generally demands or strongly suggests positions at variance with liberal and conservative stances alike. America would benefit from hearing the text's voice—diversely interpreted, of course—loud and clear, and so would we.

Indeed, the renewal of Jewish politics in this country is utterly indispensable to the community's strength. I don't believe for a moment that the future of American Jewry depends on its taking this or that particular stand on the issues of the day, and certainly not on its adopting mine. But I do not see how we can hope to revitalize either Jewish tradition or Jewish community in America if we are seen (as we often are at present, justifiably so) to take *no* stand—and thereby have our silence signify assent to the status quo. It is urgent that we demonstrate to ourselves and our children—particularly to teenagers and young adults pondering the nature and degree of their own Jewish commitments—that we are engaged as a community, with the guidance of Torah, in the work that covenant commands.

If we are serious about Torah, *tikkun olam* is non-negotiable, and if we are serious about *tikkun olam,* we must be active politically— not only as individual Jews but as a community; not only in our own names but in the name of Torah. If we don't wish to be serious, that is something else again. But in that case we should not wonder why Jewish numbers are dwindling. Keeping our heads down, playing it safe, will not win young American Jews to the cause of Torah, and should not. The only point of being Israel, as Numbers would put it, is to be counted.

Conclusion

The proper balance between grand vision and programmatic detail can never be specified in advance, never located once and for all, and never stated simply or unequivocally. That is the built-in difficulty of Jewish politics, the challenge that can never be conquered but only met. It demands in America today an effort of investigation and reflection on our part comparable to the talmudic learning which has for centuries gone into traditional responses to the issues of the day. We need medical ethicists and Jewish policy planners. We need inter-disciplinary collaborations of all sorts, multiple centers for social action, and a plurality of institutes for Jewish research. These re-sources are imperative. For our situation is unprecedented, and so must be our politics. Only the proper balance between covenant and normalcy, located after painstaking reflection, can prevent covenan-tal politics from trampling people underfoot in God's name (as happens in Israel all too often) and prevent normal politics from sending them in a thousand different directions and hence leading them absolutely nowhere (the rule rather than the exception in America). That balance, now as ever, is hard to create.

At times (and this may be one of them) even its pursuit seems a task that is beyond us. The truly discouraging feature of the contemporary Jewish political landscape, American and Israeli, is that it is very much the product of our own collective creation. Cruel choices confront us today in both countries, and they flow directly—though not exclusively—from widely sanctioned excesses of the past two decades, in which Jews too have played a role: sometimes, as in Israel, a leading role; sometimes, as in America, a role far from negligible. Realization of responsibility for our own predicament sometimes threatens to drain us of the hope for betterment. We know ourselves, our weaknesses, our temptations, all too well. Why then even aspire to do better? Let events take their course. They always do. That is something one *can* count on.

To evade responsibility in this way, however, is not only to defy the original terms of the covenant, which left superintendence of the earth to human beings. It also goes against the Zionist insistence that Jews stop blaming God or "the nations of the world" for their history, and assume responsibility for it themselves. One of the most valuable effects of Zionism's success in creating a Jewish state, to my mind, is that Jews who have their eyes open to history are now prevented from romanticizing or idealizing the Jewish people. Jews are not innocent, any more than Americans are innocent, the point which Niebuhr made repeatedly. American Jews in particular have a voice out of all proportion to our numbers—and therefore have no one to blame but ourselves if we have not spoken loudly enough to be heard, or worked hard enough to be effective.

For all the sober realism of its politics, Numbers encourages the hope that the better in us, Jew and Gentile, *is* enough to counteract the worse. Human heads, directed toward the good and raised high to be counted, can somehow manage despite it all to shine light and confer blessing. It sounds like sermon, of course, but *has* to be true. For if it is not, the American Jewish community will surely perish— as so many predict it will—in a wilderness without promise of redemption, the leeks and onions of Egypt once more looking very good indeed.

5

⚜

Deuteronomy

LEGACIES

Scholars have long noted the stylistic distinctiveness of Deuteronomy as compared with the other four books of the Torah: the unified and sustained exposition moving clearly from beginning to middle to end, the measured cadences and calculated repetitions, the single narrative voice. There is also a substantive shift evident in the book, however, a function of the fact that the people of Israel are about to cross the Jordan and come home—and Moses is about to take leave of them. He stares in Deuteronomy into the distance of God's promise, and stares at the very same moment into his own immediate foreground, the grave. His language takes on special urgency because it must stop where his feet do, on the far side of the river. When this speech ends, so will his life. Hence the repeated appeals to Israel to listen, really listen, as if life and death depended on it, for they do. "Hear, O Israel!" The message must be pared down to essentials, utterly clear, capable of being not only understood but passed on. At the end of Moses' life, and the end of Torah, the focus shifts from *observance* of the covenant to its *transmission,* from the detail of ritual and social order (though Deuteronomy certainly cares about these) to the more difficult matter of making them an inheritance for future generations. The meaning of Torah moves, in a word, from *law* to *teaching*; the main business of the day is education.

American Jewry has of late been seized by a similar concern with "continuity" (and therefore with education), prompted in part by the aging of the generation of communal leadership which lived through the Holocaust, the creation of the State of Israel, and the subsequent rise of the Jewish community in this country to unprecedented wealth and achievement. In our case too anxiety about continuity has led to intense reflection on what it is that we wish to continue—and what we have achieved that is *worthy* of continuing. All of us of course ask these questions individually as well. The Jewish calendar structures such reflection every year as Rosh Hashanah and Yom Kippur approach (and places us through the cycle of Torah readings in the company of Moses as we do so). It often happens, too, that the questions take us by surprise: stimulated by the death of a friend, perhaps, or a bout with illness or disease, or a particularly stunning sunset, or a look on the faces of our children. It suddenly becomes urgent to know whether we have achieved anything in our lives that is worthy of emulation, or learned anything in our journeys through life that truly merits passing on. And this reflection sometimes casts doubt on the ability to do good or confer blessing. How "transform the world into the kingdom of God," as the Jewish prayerbook demands, when our own needed self-transformation is so laggard, and awareness of our many imperfections so overwhelming? How teach students, raise kids, when we are not sure whether we ourselves have yet learned what we most need to know?

My purpose in this concluding chapter, following the lead of Moses' concluding orations in Deuteronomy, is reflection on what we as Jewish individuals and communities in contemporary America should be trying to pass on as the legacy of our generation. I take it as a given, following the text, that personal renewal is indispensable to collective efforts toward repair of the world. I assume too, again following Moses, that we as individuals cannot undertake the goals set by Torah unless we are convinced that they are both worthwhile and (to some degree at least) achievable. The promise of the covenant must stand clearly in front of us every step of the way—and stand before us concretely, not as a matter for generations we will never see, but as a matter of life and death to us and to those closest to us. Finally, I presume that the issue is not prophecy but meaning: that what we as individuals and communities need to know, when concerned with continuity, is the significance of *what is and has been* rather than the facts of *what will be*.

The point, as in Deuteronomy, is not the shape of the future, but the nature, the import, of the present. "Take to heart these words which I command you this day, and teach them to your children" (6:6). The message to be taught is one which we should already have learned, from Moses and from life. But what, pared down to unforgettable essentials, is it? And how can the teaching of the message be accomplished so well that our students and children take it with them into realities very different from any that we ourselves have known?

Adulthood as a Vocation

Deuteronomy both facilitates the task of education and makes it immeasurably more difficult.

It facilitates teaching in that the message of the book is clear, the language soaring, the focus on education pronounced, the task set for it worthy of any lifetime. We are to translate the words of Torah—*devarim*—into things, facts on the ground, social realities—*devarim* in the other sense of the word—which testify to the truth of the covenant rather than against it.

However, the book also complicates the work of education immensely by insisting that the good we can achieve and know through the life of mitzvah is always far from straightforward. Indeed, any hope that we can actually make it to the fulfillment of God's promise will inevitably be disappointed. The text's talk of a time when poverty will disappear is followed within several short verses by regulations for dealing with the poverty that will never disappear (15:4, 7). Moses' picture of ideal fulfillment in chapter 26 gives way immediately to a litany of curses so vivid they drive all memory of blessing from the reader's mind. And near the very end, as if even this degree of sobriety were inadequate to the facts that we must confront and surmount, Moses is told by God as he prepares to die that his people will soon "go astray after the alien gods in their midst, in the land that they are about to enter" (31:16). God has for some reason chosen not to destroy these gods, but has rather allowed them to flourish in the land of milk and honey designated for the fulfillment of the covenant. "They will forsake Me and break My covenant that I made with them." The gap between expectations and outcomes—ever on Moses' mind in the Torah because it is repeatedly evinced by the facts—is more immense at the close than ever.

Far from worrying overmuch about that discrepancy, however,

much less denying it, Deuteronomy in fact makes the point a central theme. The book is apparently determined that its readers face up to what we are all up against in trying to make the world, and ourselves, better. Its honesty is at once discouraging—for why should we try, if we are bound to fail?—and bracing, compelling, profound. It certainly gains the book a hearing (the avowed intention) that a more sentimental or utopian portrayal of the human condition would not.

On the one hand, we see and sympathize with a leader who, at the end of his life, cannot and does not expect the Israelites to become paragons of virtue any time soon, or the nations to emulate their commandments—though that is precisely the promise held out in chapter 4. Moses would not shout, "Hear, O Israel!" so repeatedly if he were not aware that human beings as a rule do not listen. When he devotes a mere fourteen verses (28:1–14) to the blessings which will come the people's way if they heed his words, and lavishes over fifty on the curses that they will suffer if they do not (vv. 16–68), we know that he knows the score. We have all learned a lot about hell on earth by middle age, and have seen far too little of heaven. Moses' ratio seems, on reflection, about right.

On the other hand, though—and far more important, the book would say—the promise is real. The possibility of achieving it has been provided and guaranteed: the path of mitzvah is meant for human beings, rather than angels, to walk. It is not in heaven, Moses declares, not across the sea, but close by, in the heart, to do. "See, I set before you this day life and goodness, death and evil. . . . Choose life, so that you and your descendants may live!" (30:15,19). The text wants neither blindness to the fact of immense obstacles nor the paralysis sometimes induced by the presence of those obstacles. It wants us to remember always that we are still on the Jordan's far side, distant from realization of the promise, but to know as well that we can cross over and inherit blessing. Some good is possible, and every act of goodness carries its own reward. The ultimate consequences of our actions lie way beyond vision—in the deeds of children of children, students of students. And besides, what choice do we have? This is the good, after all. This *is* life, and the purpose of life. The other way offers certain death. We all know that.

The command to choose life and the good is perhaps the most fundamental mitzvah that the Torah ever enunciates, and not only because it is the obvious prerequisite to fulfillment of all others (no commandments can be performed by the dead). Its importance lies in the fact that it echoes—at the conclusion of the Torah, and in decidedly moral terms—the command of *physical* procreation with which God blessed the first human beings at creation, the very beginning, when God pronounced them and their world "very good" and humanity had not yet acquired the "knowledge of good and evil." The command to *choose* the good thereby emphasizes, even more than the rest of Torah, that the good and evil which we do in this world are *of ultimate value*, part of the divine plan for creation—for why else would God bother with them? It presumes, further, that human beings are, to some degree at least, *capable of obedience*—for why else would God have made the covenant with us?

Given Deuteronomy's failure to speculate on other realities, worlds beyond this one—"the secret things belong to God," it proclaims—we cannot escape the conundrum of intentions and outcomes posed in the text by postulating another realm where all the evil in this world—hurricanes and cancer, plagues and the prosperity of the wicked—is somehow made okay. *This* world can be made good, the text insists; and it can be made good in *our* terms, good as we know good, not in some unknown divine sense which transmutes apparent evil into virtue and makes horrible suffering worthwhile. We can never know the precise measure of our actions' value because we do not know how things will ultimately turn out. "The secret things belong to God" in this sense as in others. But—the text holds fast to the paradox—"the revealed things belong to us, and to our children, forever, to do all the *devarim* of this Torah" (29:28). The meaning of our actions is here for us, every day: not in the heavens, as the text puts it, not across the sea, but here.

This is to me a powerful message. It says that being overflows with significance that we can grasp at but cannot master or comprehend. Precisely *because* intentions so often go awry, *because* unintended consequences seem to flow from every action great and small, *because* the effects of our actions are felt to the third and fourth generation, the achievements of a lifetime not knowable until played out in the lives of children and grandchildren, students and the students of students—precisely because of all that, the good and evil chosen every moment must be known to have their own intrinsic reward, as well as to carry with them effects in the future which cannot possibly be calculated. There is a more ultimate consolation as well. Deuter-onomy does want to reassure us, as God reassures Moses, that history will eventually conform to the divine plan for it. Someday goodness will assuredly result in further goodness. In a word—unknown to the Torah, but implicit in it—the messiah will come. But the *meantime* is the reality relevant to Deuteronomy, as to us—and in the meantime it is the shape of the present and not the future which is of concern. The present must be perceived correctly, its possibilities seized. Real good and evil, actual life and death, are in our hands. There is work to be done.

The content of that work, the means and focus of correct perception, are articulated in a second crucial passage in Deuteronomy's theory of the adult vocation: the *ve'ahavta* (6:5–9). Means and end are both comprised in *love*. I never paid attention before becoming a parent to the fact that the verse generally recognized as the credo of Jewish faith and therefore placed by the rabbis at the heart of every prayer service—the *Shema Yisrael*: "Hear, O Israel, the Lord is our God, the Lord is one"—is followed immediately by the injunction to "love the Lord your God with all your heart and all your soul and all your might," and then, without pause, by the command to educate the next generation:

> These words which I command you this day shall be upon your heart. You shall teach them to your children and speak of them when you sit in your home and when you walk on the way, when you lie down and when you rise up. Bind them as a sign upon your hand and let them serve as a symbol on your forehead; inscribe them on the doorposts of your house and on your gates. (6:4–9)

Love is the means as well as the end of parenting, the key to making the world a place in which life is chosen and good an activity so palpably worthwhile that it puts to rest all question of its value. We expect as much, by this point in life and in the Torah. Love reframes the questions of value, success, and results. It overcomes the gap between expectations and outcomes, enabling one to "choose life" without reservation. We do not ask, regarding love of children, "What for? What good will it do?" The experience of love has the ability to convince us—in a way which even the words of the Torah cannot—of its own self-sufficient correctness.

Much of Deuteronomy's particular approach to love has been

prefigured in Leviticus. Its emphasis falls upon behavior rather than feelings, of course, and particularly upon the pervasive and persuasive instruction conveyed by everyday realities. The facts inside which we live offer more powerful testimonies concerning love than any words, divine or human, which we could utter. *Devarim* in the latter sense cannot compete with *devarim* in the former. "Gates and doorposts"—the bounds of public and private life—must therefore be marked and ordered in such a way as to make God's commandments plausible. For everything testifies: widows and orphans lacking a protector or finding one, false and true weights and measures in the marketplace, corrupt and honest judgments in the courts. That is the reason why a law-code stands at the center of Deuteronomy (chapters 12–25). Everything testifies. Love and its absence both declare themselves through action.

With kids this is particularly the case. My children constantly ask me why I've done things I didn't realize I was doing. They noticed even if I did not. I am astonished to hear them repeating verbatim entire sentences I've uttered days before—including words I'd rather not have them know. Whenever I don't give money to a homeless person on the street they demand an explanation. Every action or omission conveys some message that our children receive, and that is all the more true of minute interactions with them, multiplied by the tens of thousands every year. We either teach Torah or something else at every moment, "when we lie down and when we rise up." If we do not teach Torah enough of the time, the opposite of Torah will prevail in the world—Deuteronomy's worst nightmare and, now that I am a parent, mine.

The text's emphasis upon the home, seen in this light, seems entirely reasonable. Home remains, even now when we spend so much time outside of it, the center of the moral self's activity and so of its concern. It is the place where we are most ourselves, least the creatures of the roles we so often play; the place, too, where we most often act out the choices we have made between blessing and curse, good and evil, in full view of our children. Masks down, tie and jacket stowed, ordinariness the rule, we find out what we are like when character is tested, learn what, if anything, we have to give, see the extent and limits of our love. This is precious knowledge and it comes no other way. Secrets deeply buried in the psyche act themselves out every day in routine behavior observable to any eye trained to notice it. Home is the daily battleground where theory and practice skirmish, and so the place where the Torah's words are most often heeded, stifled, distorted, or ignored. Deuteronomy takes a child's-eye view: unimpressed by books that he or she cannot read, but impressed for life by what goes on about the house, material for therapy ever after.

Consider in this connection Deuteronomy's reprise of the Ten Commandments given originally in Exodus. Not only do we honor or dishonor parents at home, and perform the majority of traditional Sabbath observances there, we also learn to lie, to steal goods and reputations that do not belong to us (I follow the rabbis' figurative interpretation of theft), and of course to covet. Little kids are big on coveting. Their desires, unlike ours, are wonderfully explicit. Gates and doorposts also mark the site, and bear the stain, of our adulteries. Home is the locus of much violence and a significant proportion of all homicides. Small wonder that Deuteronomy believes it is the place where its ideals—or their opposites, idolatries of self or wealth or power—will be most graphically displayed.

The Torah intends us to work *through* the realm of daily decision-making on the path to God and goodness, rather than around it. Any path on which Deuteronomy cares to lead us involves self-knowledge gained the hard way, through painful experience. Wisdom in the Torah's view is not conferred in blissful isolation. We learn it through interactions with others, and particularly from those with whom we are most intimate. In significant measure, the wisdom both comes through and consists in acts of love. We learn most from those who love us most—parents, spouses, friends—and learn not least from the pain that inevitably accompanies that love.

A friend of mine put it this way, in a letter that I quote with her permission:

> This business of raising kids is not so simple. [My teenage daughter] has lately taken to explaining with varying degrees of anger and contempt exactly how I fail as a mother and a human being. . . . She honestly thinks she is bringing me news: that I don't know I transform pain into anger, that my kids are frequently scared by it. . . . She doesn't understand compassion yet—or forgiveness. But the truth is I wasn't able to be compassionate to or separate from my parents until I was thirty years old. . . . The main point is that being a parent is the hardest thing I have ever done in my entire life. Sometimes I feel racked by the

enormity of the demands—the physical demands, the emotional demands, the intellectual demands, the EMOTIONAL demands. Who expected it to be so complicated?

Not me, certainly. I too figured, sometime in my twenties, that I had a pretty good idea of what my parents had done wrong. I would simply work hard to avoid repeating their mistakes. Marriage might be difficult, but not child rearing. I guess I should have paid more attention to my piano teacher, who with the compassion of adulthood always told me it was alright to make mistakes so long as they were different from the ones I'd made the week before—for I always would make mistakes. I had no idea of the emotional power inherent in the relationship to one's kids. Reason often flies out the window. One feels in the grip of primal forces one can only wrestle with but never control. Voices take over that I did not know I had inside me.

> I love each of my kids [my friend continues] with an intensity that would frighten them out of their wits if they knew. I find myself staring at the back of —'s neck or —'s wrist or —'s forehead with total absorption, trying to memorize their shape against the knowledge that one day they will live elsewhere and I won't be able to recall that detail. I wonder if my mother felt the same way about me.

Deuteronomy, I think, means to capture precisely this intense *physicality* of relation through its frequent resort to concrete metaphor. It compares the heeding of God's word to a path through the wilderness (8:2–6) because such a path, in a wilderness without signposts, is of life and death importance. Manna, food from heaven, is used to teach that human beings do not "live by bread alone"— because without food we die and because eating is our primary mode of healthy relation with the world outside our bodies. We too get life and truth mouth to mouth, as it were, just as Moses did from God.

Ever focused on the intensity and intimacy of this instruction in the home, Deuteronomy is relentless in linking means to ends, medium to message. Love is the curriculum as well as the goal of proper parenting. That is at once a truism and a challenge to our usual behavior. We all know that our *devarim* in the two senses of words and things should be conjoined, that love of God with "heart, soul and might" needs to be taught to children night and day, by exhibiting it in as many circumstances as possible. The way to love, like Israel's march through the wilderness, is pursued only by walking it and not by preaching or describing it. We know too that it is not self-evident how to do this—or easy to do once we know how. All of us require people whose love we can emulate—friends, spouses, parents—as well as more systematic guidance in acquiring the skills required to receive love, as to give it. We must learn about love from them, if we are to teach as we should.

> [My wife] is now sleeping on the couch [writes another friend]. . . . She has been my teacher about love since college. . . . Left to my own devices, I'm basically a selfish son of a bitch. Matter of fact, I think that's part of what the people who really love me (like you) have always responded to. It's not news that narcissism can be attractive and powerful. Giving it up has not been easy. What I did not know in college is that love means caring for someone else's feelings. Profound, huh? This also suggests that it helps if you understand that there is really someone else on the other end of a relationship. Unfortunately, if these truths are not held to be self-evident at the outset, to learn them requires some major renovation. I'm not sure why [my wife] bothered to take on such a slow learner.

Relationships to children particularly demand this learning. In theory, love for them should come easily. The Torah does not bother to command it. Our kids after all adore us. And since we are so identified with them, love ourselves in loving them, narcissism too seems to be in love's service. In practice, however, as every parent knows, one must struggle to meet and not resent the "emotional demands" capitalized by the first friend I quoted, writing in desperation at their relentlessness. Self-love is not a reliable vehicle for good parenting. It's one thing to experience "love of having the good for oneself always" with one's children, and quite another to enact love daily and nightly as empathy, care, patience, tending. The needs often occupy so much foreground that the reward for meeting them is put off into the background or even moves out of the picture altogether. Yet giving love this way is far from self-sacrifice. We know this. Knowing it, we do choose life and the good for our children, every day, in spite of everything.

The interdependence of our various loves is no less fundamental to Deuteronomy's vision. It is folly to talk about goodness in the community or the world unless it flourishes in the home. Nor is love a zero-sum game. One does not have less love for one's spouse but more thanks to loving one's children. Love inside the family need not compete with love of friends—and none of these competes with love of God, heart and soul and might. The Torah rather assumes that we cannot give love to God *unless* we have learned to love the human beings closest to us—just as we cannot fully love each other, in the Torah's view, without the centeredness, the direction, the ultimate grounding, which only connection to God can provide. This too is at the core of the curriculum I hope to pass on to my children: work toward the kind of selfhood which the Torah describes and makes possible. I hope they will achieve it to a greater degree than their father.

Consider the Ten Commandments one final time, then, not as a code of social mores or an order for a loving home but as a set of instructions in *becoming an authentic self,* a kind of schooling in the vocation of adulthood. I realize of course that they are far more than that. The Torah wishes *us* to serve *God* and not the other way around. But its point—and mine here—is precisely that the two sorts of service are not mutually exclusive. To this end the text pictures a relation to God, in community, that confers a depth of self which in its view is not otherwise available.

God begins instruction in this truth by letting us know who is speaking: the Parent who created us, the Teacher who set us on our wilderness journey, the One beyond image or comprehension who can nonetheless be present in this world and confer ultimate value upon it. Thanks to God's ultimate grounding, we are (or can be) "out of Egypt," the "narrow place" of bondage and affliction. Freed of external oppression, we have space in which to grow into independent selves. "Freedom from," as the political theorists put it, is the precondition of every meaningful "freedom to."

To be free means not having other gods "on the face" of this God—no specious ultimates interposing themselves between us and the ultimate reality, hiding it, keeping us from immediate relation to it, and thus enslaving us as surely as Pharaoh. Encounter with the "Eternal Thou," as with all human "thous," proceeds directly, "face to face." For the same reason, we cannot afford to make false representations of the ultimate and then accord them ultimate authority, "bow down to them." That too would distract us from the

pursuit of integrity, our search for oneness that reflects God's. Service
to what is less than ultimate leaves its mark on children and grandchildren. Love and goodness, however obscurely, make a mark "to
the thousandth generation." Authentic personal fulfillment has more
than the individual self at stake.

Hence the third command: that we not "raise up the name of the
Lord your God to nothing" [meaning literally: not swear falsely]—
thereby bringing what is highest all the way down to nothingness.
God "will not forgive" a self who does such a thing, for human
selfhood will simply not survive the total confusion of above with
below. We all want truth, not falsehood; we want life, not nothingness. We do not want to mistake one for the other, and we cannot
afford to act as if they were not distinct. How choose life, or love, if
we do?

The Sabbath, a weekly remembrance of creation, is meant to help
us avoid that mistake, not least because it is linked explicitly, in
Deuteronomy's recitation of the commandments, to redemption from
Egypt. No servile work: so that we can remember our freedom to go
higher. No resignation to the servitude of others: lest we lose confidence that we *can* go higher, our hope threatened when we see others
condemned to settle for much less than the stature for which they
were created. No confusion of creature with Creator, lest we forget
that we are commanded to complete the work of Creation, in our
own selves first of all, in accordance with a design that precedes and
transcends us. Its prerequisite, we are reminded here, is freedom.

No surprise, then, that the Torah proceeds from the ultimate
Creator to our proximate creators, parents, and urges respect for
them as well. Make them as weighty as we ourselves would like to be.
Human beings become weighty by investing honor in people and
causes worthy of it. That seems obvious enough. But we also become
weighty by overcoming the most powerful resistances to love, working through the most powerful ambivalences which come with love.
The world did not require Freud to discover that these lie in our
relations to our parents. Honor them, the text urges, in order that
"your days be long, and it be good for you, in the land which the Lord
your God gives you"; that is, in the land of promise, the place where
we all want our children to live after us. Such honor for parents, this
being the Torah, is of course not a feeling or an attitude but a pattern
of behavior.

There is to be no murder, no adultery or theft, for obvious reasons. We all have to learn to resist the temptation to try to grasp hold of life by squeezing it out of others. Ernest Becker's reflections on the evils which result from our "denial of death" are apposite here. That denial, he argues, is most often attempted by lording it over others, building the self up at their expense.[1] We all have the power to confirm selfhood or destroy it, confer security or rob it, and exercise it every day. We never seem to get as much self as we need in this life, or to give as much as we should. But we are so constituted, the Torah insists, that authentic selfhood is possible—if we have the proper relation to the ultimate source of dignity and to its proximate sources, our families and communities.

There is no authenticity, by definition, without truth. No false witness against the neighbor, therefore. The point as always is *true* witness, in life as well as words. Little things point to big ones, express big ones: another Freudian truth presumed here by Deuteronomy.

Finally, as climax to all the rest, and the highest ideal of all, there is the command not to covet the "neighbor's wife," or to lust after anything that belongs to others. Love must not be servant to desire. The tenth commandment describes the supreme achievement: selves so in love with God and the world, so completely fulfilling the command to choose life—as it is, as we are, with exactly the things and the loves we have, and no more—that we are entirely satisfied within the limits assigned us. No one can fully obey this commandment. Moses too fails miserably. He is mortal, after all. But we can, like him, glimpse the end of the journey, the contours of the promised land. We know what authentic selfhood would look like, and can aim for it.

"Hear this, O Israel," the book proclaims. Authentic selfhood is possible. God and family, friends and community, are means to it rather than obstacles. Love, guided by Torah, is sufficient to nurture healthy and good human beings. It can be done! Despite everything, despite the inevitable failures, the tragedies you can control and those you cannot. The love in circulation all around us proclaims itself enough and more than enough, in need of no further reason for existence. It gives us the strength to defy the horrors in the world and choose life and the good. Meaning cannot be comprehended by us, Deuteronomy believes, but it is assured. Our job is not to complete the work of "inheriting" the promised land but only to model for our children the love Torah describes and makes possible, so that they can know and model it in turn.

One final virtue must be inculcated if love is to be free to do this work: courage in the face of suffering and death. Deuteronomy repeatedly calls on the Israelites to keep their eyes fixed on the promise ahead, and to remember the blessings which have come their way. Only so can they overcome the curses. We ourselves perform a parallel labor of confidence building when we hold on tight to the examples of our friends' good lives, their happy marriages, and healthy children—and to the hope that our children might enjoy lives better still. It's not easy to remember these or any good things, amid the many awful negatives in experience. With a child on one's lap, though, or a friend close by, one can often succeed in banishing anxiety, and not fear the time when our children will have to walk the path without us.

"Be strong and of good courage," Moses urges Joshua, his true heir among the children of Israel. "Fear not, and be not dismayed" (30:7–8). This seems to me the hardest of all the lessons that an adult has to learn. I still struggle with it. Year after year I watch Moses reckon with his imminent death and am amazed at his seeming acceptance. I am grateful, reading these verses in late summer, that, God willing, I will have another year in which to work on *my* acceptance. Rosh Hashanah, another chance, is imminent. By middle-age we generally do not require the Torah cycle to bring the matter of death to mind. We watch our parents retire, age, deal with sickness on a chronic basis, die. We parent in place of our parents, and mourn friends lost to cancer, AIDS, or early heart attacks. We have perhaps even witnessed the special pain which comes when friends lose their children and have to say *kaddish* in their place: the exact opposite of how things are meant to be. The power to love is strained by such events. Courage is sorely tested. Energy for work in the world is put on hold or undermined.

Part of this begins, I think [writes a friend], with my mother's death. [I was going through her things about a month ago,] confronted by eight sets of china, four or five dozen dresses . . . hot trays, toasters, perfume and toiletries. . . . What I was struck most by was the simple futility of the whole thing. All these objects with no home or purpose except to burden me after her death. And how amazing that, knowing this, I am doing exactly the same thing!

My first reaction to your question "what about the course of your life has most surprised you?" [writes another friend] was—nothing. Things have gone pretty much according to schedule. . . . However, my next thought was my father's death. That wasn't supposed to happen. . . . Your question touches on the relationship between surprise, choice, and fate. That which was not supposed to happen, which surprises you, becomes that which determines your fate? Hence, my vow to be in shape by my fortieth birthday and my now regular trips to our spiffy new health club. I guess what I'm saying is that I don't know what my life would look like if my father were still alive. Would I have felt the world contained more options, or fewer? I know that I would be basically the same person, me (whoever that is), although I suspect some parts of myself, or rather the course of my life, would be very different.

It's hard to know; my parents are still alive, thank God, a fact that has certainly made all the difference in my life. But I can well understand the hours of *shiva* my friends have spent pondering the destiny imposed by their parents and trying to work through the ambivalence of their relation. I too have been prompted more than once, by the loss of friends who died young, to consideration of the world's lack of fairness. Defiance of death may well be the least of the affirmations we need to make if we are to progress on Deuteronomy's life-path of mitzvah. For me, however, it is perhaps the hardest—and, I think, not only for me. Fifty years after the Holocaust, two hundred years into the profoundly secular culture of the modern West, and with all of us exposed without cease, thanks to television, to the sight of war and murder—the "death question," as Saul Bellow calls it, has taken on special urgency. Perhaps, as he seems to suggest in his fiction, it has also taken on special menace.

Deuteronomy, true to form, refuses to alleviate anxiety on this score—personal or collective—with the comforts of another world. It is utterly silent on the subject of what awaits Moses beyond the grave. "The secret things belong to God" in this matter most of all. The book says what can be said, according to its experience of God and the world, and no more. I think, however, that the book's many affirmations—of life itself, of love, of authentic selfhood in just community with God—leave us with a powerful interrogative: why *not* believe that these goods do not end with life as we know it?

Here too we stand before a choice. One can think of death as the irretrievable loss of absolutely everything and act accordingly. "These same conclusions," Bellow writes in *Humboldt's Gift,* "were incorporated into the life of society and present in all its institutions, in politics, education, banking, justice." *Or* one could think otherwise. "Suppose, however, that oblivion is not the case?" Bellow's character Charlie Citrine confesses a "lifelong intimation" to this effect that is either "a tenacious illusion or else the truth deeply buried."[2]

Deuteronomy seeks to stimulate a similar intimation in its readers. The book never speculates and never preaches about the reality for which it has no words. Yet the rabbis were not wrong to infer a suggestion in its pages of a larger whole, a reality still more enduring than heaven and earth. To be free from the weight of death liberates energy, Charlie avers. It gives one "an overflow to be good with."[3] That is Deuteronomy's intention exactly.

From this, courage flows. I myself rarely get it from words, even the Torah's words. It comes rather from countervailing facts in my experience: from the children to whom I have transmitted life, and wish to transmit good; the love of my wife and friends; experiences of just and caring community; astonishing encounters with the kindness of strangers. All these convey the assurance that life is good. Death is not good—but (if it comes in old age) it might be okay. One can live with it. The path we are on is the right one, despite all its inadequacies and ours and those our children too will soon manifest. Walking this path is supremely, self-evidently worthwhile. From this confidence to be and to love comes the ability to take responsibility for some corner of the world and try to transform it: to choose life and the good. It gives rise as well to the sense that one has in fact learned something worthy of transmission, and might through example be able to pass it on.

Educating Jews

Accomplishing this is of course the business of education—and there seems to be widespread consensus that no task is more urgent for the revitalization of Jewish community and tradition in America today than overhauling the aims and methods of Jewish education. There also seems to be considerable agreement on the steps needed to achieve this reform: the concrete matters of curricula, finances, teacher-training, and the like. I shall not discuss those matters here because they are a subject of some consensus, and in any case require specialized expertise which I do not possess. I will try instead to lay out the *principles* which I think should guide Jewish educational reform, a vision of where (according to my reading of the Torah) we should be going, what legacy we should be leaving as a community for the generations to follow.[4]

My starting point—a truism when one works in the framework of Deuteronomy—is the conviction that any Jewish theory of education, and certainly any theory of Jewish education, cannot but begin with Torah. Jewish education is trying to carry forward the conversation begun at Sinai, to apply the words (*devarim*) of Torah to the ever-new circumstances (*devarim*) of Jewish life. This move from path to pathlessness, like the others described in this book, must therefore root itself firmly in the tradition of Jewish thought and history on the subject. I shall therefore couch my discussion of Jewish education in terms provided by modern Jewish thinkers who have preceded us on the stretch of wilderness we are still walking two centuries after it began. Six principles, suggested by these thinkers, are to my mind fundamental.

The first—that Jewish education must change radically to take account of our unprecedented situation—is highlighted in the text which inaugurated the corpus of modern Jewish thought: Moses Mendelssohn's *Jerusalem* (1783), a book which, among other things and perhaps above other things, is also the first text of modern Jewish educational theory. For me the key point comes in the startling page near the start of the second "theological" section of *Jerusalem,* where Mendelssohn talks about the immense damage done to the world by the multiplication of books. "We teach and instruct one another only through writings," he complains. "We learn to know nature and man only from writings. We work and relax, edify and amuse ourselves through overmuch writing. . . . The professor reads his written lectures from the chair. Everything is dead letter; the spirit of living conversation has vanished. . . . Hence, it has come to pass that man has almost lost his value for his fellow man." The passage concludes with one final lament: "we do not need the man of experience; we only need his writings. In a word, we are literati, men of letters. Our whole being depends on letters; we can scarcely comprehend how a mortal man can educate and perfect himself without a book."[5]

If we take Mendelssohn seriously, as I do, we have to wonder what lies behind this cantankerous and transparently exaggerated, even facile, argument. One does not expect such reactionary sentiment from Mendelssohn, an apostle of enlightenment and reason who can usually be counted on for nuanced judgment and judicious expression. When he denounces words and books in a book crafted with such consummate care that it marks a turning point in the history of Jewish thought, a book that is only one of many written in the course of a long, productive, and extremely verbal life, we know that something important must be going on.

It is; Mendelssohn is reckoning with the consequences of his argument in part one of *Jerusalem* that neither state nor church nor synagogue had any right to exercise coercion upon the thought or actions of any religious adherent. His theory of education welcomes and plans for the fact—discussed at length in the first chapter of this essay—that henceforth commitment by Jews to Judaism would have to be *voluntary, partial, and pluralist.* Good and powerful reasons would have to be provided in order to persuade Jews to choose Judaism. Every student in his time, Mendelssohn wrote, had become overly dependent upon books, because he no longer had the ability to "follow his teacher, to watch him, to observe all his actions, and to obtain the instruction which he was capable of acquiring by means of his talents, and of which he had rendered himself worthy by his conduct."[6]

In the ideal state of affairs, *social reality* would be the classroom, lived experience the text. "In everything a youth saw being done, in all public as well as private dealings, on all gates and on all doorposts, in whatever he turned his eyes or ears to, he found occasion for inquiring and reflecting."[7] The echoes of the *ve'ahavta* in that formulation are apparent. And Mendelssohn's warning about the difficulty of educating Jews in the absence of Jewish gates and doorposts has proven all too prescient. The situation he describes is still our Jewish present, and will remain the Jewish future. Jewish learning must clearly take a different course than it has in any era heretofore.

Franz Rosenzweig, charting his vision of that course in the famous dialogue with Martin Buber to which we referred in chapter 1, found it necessary to criticize all of the nineteenth-century options for Jewish commitment created in the wake of Mendelssohn's *Jerusalem*. "From Mendelssohn on, our entire people has subjected itself to the torture of this embarrassing questioning; the Jewishness of every individual has squirmed on the needle point of a 'why'" (238). Better to stop worrying about systems and rationales, whether Orthodox or Reform, Rosenzweig urged, and to start probing for the personal meaning which Buber had called "inner power." We have discussed these ideas at some length and need not review them here.

The main point of his argument, however, does merit repetition: Rosenzweig's notion of the leap from "path" to "pathlessness," which articulates what I consider the essentials of Jewish learning, and of Jewish living, in our day. All of us must repeatedly leave the paved roads which comprise the Judaisms—and the lives—known thus far. As we turn pages on the calendar never before reached, we come to situations and dilemmas that demand unprecedented response. If we want to respond *as Jews,* venturing onto pathlessness in a way that continues the path (really the set of paths) called Judaism, our response must come in terms of what Jewish traditions have taught before us. When we leap into pathlessness as learned Jews, we carry the traditions of Torah along with us. Judaism is thereby preserved, kept vital in and through us.

A Judaism which has nothing to say to the lives Jews actually lead, nothing to add to the arts and sciences and professions of our day, nothing to resolve the dilemmas of morality or policy, is a Judaism that has ceased to be itself, ceased to be Torah. It has become nostalgia, sentiment, at best a literature with a place of honor in the history of human development. But how enable Torah to be more than that, how have it speak to new situations, except by enabling it to speak through Jews who have taken its manifold teachings into themselves and are embarked on what Rosenzweig called the "laborious and aimless detour through knowable Judaism"?[8] Such Jews do not for a moment leave behind all they are and know from the worlds in which their days are actually spent. Nor do they know in advance what Torah will command in a situation never before confronted. This is what Rosenzweig meant by a

> new sort of learning . . . a learning in reverse order. A learning that no longer starts from the Torah and leads into life, but the other way round: *from* life, from a world that knows nothing of the Law, or pretends to know nothing, back to the Torah. That is the sign of the time.[9]

It still is, I believe, and will remain so. The purpose of Jewish learning is precisely the living dialogue that Rosenzweig described between groups of Jews in all their variety and the set of traditions that have their source in Torah. Ideally, Jews will all belong to communities in the strong sense of that word described in chapter 3: people bound to one another in bonds of obligation and even affection. Only inside such communities are individuals able to learn and teach through the method of inner power, leaping from path to pathlessness by wrestling honestly, openly, and as whole selves with the issues they cannot not address. I believe that this dialogue in fact *is* Torah, whenever we do it seriously.

Jewish schools, in the absence of confirming social reality, have to work all the harder at bringing Jews of all ages to the tables around which this Torah is learned and taught. The more tables the better; the more diverse the tables, the better; the more diverse the people around them, the better, both for us and for Torah. Jewish feminists have proven this beyond any doubt in recent years, if any proof was needed. The growing divergence between American and Israeli Judaisms offers another example, another gift.

Rosenzweig established the Frankfurt Lehrhaus, a center of adult education, because he knew, as we should, that the tables where Torah grows cannot be populated only by the young. We are on a path which does not "give him who had traveled its whole length the right to say that he had now arrived at the goal." It is not a matter of books to read, curricula to cover. Does this any longer require arguing? Torah, like the good, is accomplished only by doing it repeatedly, and like truth is never entirely accomplished until the messiah. We begin with the young because life does, but we fail if we end with the young—and actually sin in doing so, because we convey the false message that the Torah is more limited than life, more easily mastered, instead of the other way around. We know what happens in the vast majority of cases when we try to make active, concerned Jews of children whose parents care very little about the tradition. We fail.

Buber, spelling out the *process* in which Jewish learning should occur, its proper medium, also gave succinct expression to its message. What the Bible has to tell us, he wrote,

> what no other voice in the world can teach us with such simple power, is that there is truth and there are lies, and that human life cannot persist or have meaning save in the decision in behalf of truth and against lies; that there is right and wrong, and that the salvation of man depends on choosing what is right and rejecting what is wrong; and that it spells the destruction of our existence to divide our life up into areas where the discrimination between truth and lies, right and wrong holds, and others where it does not. . . . [10]

It is a magnificent passage, I believe, and points to an essential of Jewish education as Deuteronomy would have it proceed: namely that the Jewish school not be a space in which division holds but rather one where wholeness is not only taught but practiced and modeled. Two implications of this norm seem to me crucial. The first is that we should not be interested in educating only the Jewish half of a hyphenated self. Our tradition does not address or demand only *parts* of a person. God is to be served with *"all* your heart, soul, and might," not merely with the Jewish part, whatever that might be.

Indeed—the second implication—Buber held (again rightly, I think) that we cannot *educate* in the best sense if we rest content with only part of a self, because "what we term education . . . means to give decisive effective power to a selection of the world which is concentrated and manifested in the educator." [11] Such "effective power" means, in his terms, "Thou-ness," treating each person as an end rather than means, being fully present in interaction with him or her. In other words it presumes, as it fosters, wholeness. The child learns to trust the world, and the adult student learns to trust the tradition's authenticity and depth because the teacher who stands before them with the text in hand palpably breathes the tradition through his or her words. Only so can the selection "of what is 'right', of what should be," carry weight.

This is a tall order, of course, but it seems to me correct. Educators schooled on Deuteronomy attempt to convey confidence in the worthwhileness of life conducted along the path that they are walking.[12] They are responsible for this confidence, answerable both to the tradition that speaks through them and the students who rightly expect integrity and authenticity from those who claim to speak in the name of Torah. "Very nice," you might say. "Buber is always very nice, and even deep. But what could all this mean, in real schools? Sainthood as a prerequisite for teaching certificates? Expertise in I-Thou relations as the necessary but not sufficient condition for entry to the Jewish workplace? We do not have enough qualified teachers as it is!" Agreed—but I believe Buber's message does have a great deal of practical importance to say to us.

We should first of all heed Buber's warning that our notions of *qualification* not be misplaced. We are not merely purveying information in our classrooms. Hebrew language is not the be-all and end-all of Hebrew schools or day schools. The rudiments of Jewish history and texts, conveyed by instructors who "control" them, cannot possibly compensate for the fact that a child comes to Jewish afternoon schools for only a few hours a week, that adult learners devote even fewer hours to their Jewish learning, and that even students in day schools generally devote far less than half of their days to Jewish studies. In this, as in every other aspect of American Jewish life, the numbers are against us.

All the more reason, I would submit, to follow Buber and try our best to give children or adults, while teaching them Hebrew or history or texts, what they will rarely find in public schools or universities, in the media or on the streets, and what they have every right to expect from teachers in an institution that claims the authority of Torah: human beings who stand behind what they say; who unqualifiedly are the Jews they seem to be; who have doubts, express them, and so can all the more credibly claim that there is Truth and there is Right. Let our schools be places that hire and educate people who aspire to an integrated Jewish selfhood in which the "Jewish" is not marginal but pervasive.

Buber was right, I am afraid, when he asserted that all "education worthy of the name is essentially education of character." Let us aim to make Jewish schools places where the claim to be providing education of character would not be laughable. Buber was also right, I think, when he claimed that "genuine education of character is genuine education for community."[13] One cannot offer education that is worthwhile in a situation of alienation, in classes of unrelieved "it-ness," or through pedagogies of monologue never broken by real questions demanding honest rather than formulaic answers. We have done immense damage to the good name of Torah over the years by settling for all those.

The author of *I and Thou* was the first to admit that no one can live only in the I-Thou realm. No class can exist on a plane of perpetual excitement. There are meals to be prepared, math problems and texts to be mastered. But I join him in wondering whether we can any longer afford to tolerate lies in the classroom. We lie when we stipulate Jewish behaviors in which neither teachers nor students engage or expect to engage. "In the morning we do X." "On Sabbaths and Festivals we do Y." We lie when we claim that the American Jewish community, unlike the Israelites described by Leviticus or Numbers, contains no evils or impurities. And we give the lie to the seriousness of Torah when we settle for passing attention and rote performances rather than active minds and engaged emotions.

But there is a further implication to Buber's call for character and community. It is unavoidable, given the honest differences which divide Jews, that a portion of the schooling we provide cannot simply be Jewish but must honestly reflect our *conflicting interpretations of what the Torah demands*. To shy away from frank presentation of who we are or, worse, to rest content with platitudes is to deny students the wholeness I have been advocating with Buber's help. Paradoxically, the pursuit of whole selves means *divided schooling*—though it also means finding as much common ground as we possibly can, in our schools as in our communities, lest the gaps among us become unbridgeable and the community so divided that its selves cannot be whole.

Mordecai Kaplan, in *The Future of the American Jew* (1946), supplied a fourth principle which I think is essential to Jewish education in contemporary America: the need to prepare students for citizenship in our democracy, even as one prepares them for relation with the one country in which Judaism is the "primary civilization" lived by Jews: Israel.[14] I confess I used to believe the first point outdated, an obvious anachronism that Kaplan had received in the twenties from the philosopher John Dewey and that we, thanks to much progress in the meanwhile, could happily forego. Who needs to preach the virtues of democracy? They are, after all, well known.

My teaching of teenagers and college students over the years has changed my mind. I no longer believe it makes sense to try to educate the "Jew" in American Jews while leaving the "American" to other institutions. Pluralism is *our* need and, since Mendelssohn at least, it has become our norm, while America's needs and values of late are demonstrably diverse. It often seems that only the diversity itself is conveyed in public schools or universities, because it is evident on the very faces in the classroom. The norms that diversity should serve remain untaught. American Jews cannot afford this silence. We require a certain kind of society if we are to be at home in this country, and require it as well because *our* tradition demands it. Our norms proclaim that we are not responsible to and for the Jews alone. I argued this point at some length in chapter 4, and shall not repeat it here.

If we accept this understanding of Torah, however, and this description of contemporary American realities, the consequences for education are clear. We need to bring Jews to the point where they are able to say, with courage and authenticity, what the Torah as they hear it demands *of America*. This is our society; we "live its civilization," as Kaplan put it time and again. And if Judaism is, in his words, "a religio-ethical civilization to be fostered by the American Jew to the maximum degree compatible with the legitimate claims which American citizenship has upon him,"[15] let us agree with Kaplan that one of the aims of Jewish education should be to *stretch* prevailing conceptions of the "legitimate claims which American citizenship" exercises. We should at the same time be pushing ourselves to push America to live up to the ideals of its own civic religion. The Jew is incomplete if the American is neglected, shunted aside, left to others. Wholeness may have to remain ideal rather than achievement, as Deuteronomy warns. But fragmentation can never be an ideal, in the classroom or outside it.

All the more reason to appreciate the different dynamics of the search for Jewish wholeness in the State of Israel. Recent research has demonstrated that American Jewish schools offer precious little instruction in Israeli history, culture, or society. Israeli youngsters learn even less about diaspora Jews in any country because Zionist ideology has long since condemned these communities to imminent extinction. Somewhat more surprisingly, they also are not taught much in secular schools about Jewish tradition. Each side of the Israel-diaspora divide is thereby failing to take advantage of the Jews who are playing out the other of the only two viable options developed in the modern world for Jewish survival and Jewish thriving. A potentially fruitful dialogue is thereby silenced before it begins. Mutual contributions are precluded. Mutual challenges, which could be serious, are reduced to ignorant polemic. The loss— existentially, as well as educationally—is immense.

Existential concern with the inner life of Jews brings to mind a theme emphasized time and again by Abraham Heschel: that too much attention has been paid of late to the Jewish community and the individual's obligations to it (certainly the case in the present "continuity" crisis), while "the individual and his [or her] problems were ignored." Heschel argued with his usual eloquence that Judaism had to address the "vital personal question which every human being is called upon to answer, day in, day out. What shall I do with my mind, my wealth, my power?" We hear the *ve'ahavta* once again, this time with the emphasis upon the second person singular form of its imperatives.[16] Its implications for education are clear.

The force of Heschel's call was brought home to me recently when I stood at a shiva for a young man of thirty and listened to his friends and family describe what he had managed to accomplish and teach them in his short life. I found myself saying to his mother in the kitchen afterward that one test of a tradition is surely its adequacy to lives such as her son's—whether it gives them what they need to live richly and well. Judaism had done that in this man's case, thanks to parents for whom the tradition and the community are everything. But it has not done so for many others, who have not been reached or touched by live Jewish experiences, caring communities, or Jewish learning on a level worthy of their intelligence. Jewish education has to that degree failed those people—and I fear they constitute a majority of the American Jewish population.

It is true that the responsibility is theirs, as it is every adult's, to learn what they need to know in order to be good parents, spouses, or friends, just as they find—and generally pay for—the training required for their careers. The onus is certainly on Jewish parents to put their children on the way of Torah, first of all by walking it themselves. But most American Jews in the past two generations have *not* assumed that responsibility. The educational cycle presumed by Deuteronomy has been broken, in some cases for many generations. At this moment the responsibility therefore falls on the community, and particularly on Jewish educators, to "open up to them," as the Haggadah puts it: to open ourselves to them, to open the Torah to them.

We do so not by approaching Jews with demands or guilt but by making available a set of teachings that touch the core of the self. I take Heschel's famous "pedagogy of return" to mean, first, that we should meet people where they are and thus return them to the Torah. It also means, however, that the teaching itself should *constitute* such a return and not only a means to it. The "ladder of observance" of which Heschel spoke should likewise not mean that students climb to performance of more and more mitzvot, eventually attaining a level that their teachers have already reached and from which they direct them. Rather, the observances which Jewish educators teach and model—Torah study first among them—should help students to climb higher as human beings. This point, if we resolve not to leave it as mere cliché, offers a standard which can be employed, age-appropriately of course, in choosing curricula, textbooks, and lesson plans.

"To educate means to meet the inner needs, to respond to the inner goals of the child," Heschel wrote,[17] and I would add: not only of the child. Every time that I teach adults, I am asked, justifiably, "Why should we be reading this? What does it have to say to us?" There is a place for saying, as I often do, "This is part of your history, your tradition; make it part of the treasury out of which you furnish your mind and stir your heart. It should at least be on your shelf of consciousness beside George Eliot, Paul Cezanne, and Sigmund Freud." I advocated that position in chapter 1. But there is also a need to say with Deuteronomy, and I confess it comes less easily to me, "Look: you are a human being, and the business of life as we all well know is very difficult, often painful, never certain. You owe it to

yourself—not to the Jewish people, not to the Holocaust dead, not to
your ancestors near or distant, but to yourself, to the soul in you—to
encounter the norms and wisdom stored up in this Torah, unsur-
passed in the history of human civilization, and closer to you than
you know."

It would not hurt to add, soon after, "Judaism needs you: not for
your gift to Federation only, which will certainly help the Jewish
people, but for what you and you alone, if you become a serious Jew,
can add to the repertoire of Jewish possibilities that your friends can
then draw upon and that we will collectively pass on to the next
generation of learners." There is a need to talk of soul, of spirit, and
to do so without sacrifice of intellectual rigor. The hope is that those
who are prompted by such teaching to take "the leap into the
teachings" will also accept obligation to the Torah and the community that carries it, recognizing (as Exodus teaches) that what they
have chosen is precisely what has obligated them all along.

My own teaching and learning have repeatedly been stirred and
immeasurably improved by individuals whom I have encountered in
the classroom, teens and adults brimming with creativity, intelligence, and passion. They are often leaders in their fields and their
communities, "souls on fire" who have only recently begun to
appreciate that Torah is for them, and are only now deciding that *they*
shall therefore be for Torah. Such people bring home the lesson of
Pirke Avot (6:3), cited in chapter 3, that all of us learn Torah from one
another—at least one verse, one *halakha*, one expression, one letter—
and so owe each other mutual *kavod*, respect, Torah.

We often do not take full advantage of the potential stored up in
the millions of untapped American Jewish souls, I fear, because of
what Heschel called "a thirst for approbation." He referred specifi-
cally to "an eagerness to receive the approval of scientists or men of
affairs," but the problem seems to me far broader and more serious.
We descend into apologetics, preach a "religion of approval."[18] Our
anxiety on this score has been probed deeply by Joseph Soloveitchik
in his influential essay "The Lonely Man of Faith" (1965). The person

of faith in our time is doubly lonely, he writes. The eternal aloneness of a person whose faith commitments inside the covenant cannot fully be communicated to others is exacerbated in modern society by the isolation of living among secular devotion to "might" and "majesty." At a certain point, Soloveitchik says resignedly, "the dialogue between the man of faith and the man of culture comes to an end. . . . When the hour of estrangement strikes, the ordeal of [the] man of faith [whom he calls Adam the Second, the Adam of covenant] begins and he starts his withdrawal from society, from Adam the first, be he an outsider, be he himself."[19]

I think we must confront this question honestly, if we are to design Jewish schools for any foreseeable Jewish future, and of course must include Jewish women of faith in the discussion as well. It returns us to our starting point, Mendelssohn's *Jerusalem*, but this time with the hindsight of two centuries that have seen incredible blessings for Jews as well as unparalleled curses. When all is said and done—and I intentionally place this point at the end, where Deuteronomy places its litany of curses—we have to own up to the fact that Jewish schooling in America *educates Jews for Otherness, for difference*. Otherness is of course quite fashionable at the moment. Its presence is virtually de rigueur in academic grant proposals. But it remains hard to bear, difficult to learn, painful to teach.

Our students carry too much history into the classroom to be innocent in this regard. My seven-year-old already knows a lot about the Holocaust. My ten-year-old still worries about Rabin's murder. They both already know that there are terrorists who place bombs in buildings and on airplanes, not only in Israel but here in America, close to home—though Israel, and the busses they have ridden there, seem especially vulnerable. They also understand that Jews are a minority in this country—the lesson is driven home every Christmas—and that they, as observant Jews, are a minority within the minority. The Jewish adults I teach know still more about the exposure and alienation to which minorities are subject. Perhaps, having lived longer, they hope for less—in regard both to the position of Jews in this country and to their own ability to cope with the demands of substantive distinctiveness.

Soloveitchik reminds us—if we need reminding after Deuteronomy—that there are limits to what we can do to shape the larger society and that those limits will remain even with the greatest resources and the best of intentions. The general culture is not of our making; the political, economic, and social orders are far beyond our control and often our influence. Economic stability may not last; we may again face serious anti-Semitism in this country; peace may elude Israel for some time to come, and if it does come may weaken diaspora ties already far from strong. Curses, in short, may well outnumber blessings once again. A minority of 2 percent in a population fast approaching three hundred million understands that even in the best of times—which this may well be—the balance between the culture of Adam the first and our particular "covenantal faith community" is not set up in our favor.

Yet—a point Soloveitchik does not make—the realities of multicultural America also offer precious possibilities for Jewish community as for Jewish commitment. They constitute a real blessing and should markedly affect the shape of Jewish education. American Jews stand, as usual with Jews, in the middle. In the previous chapter, I alluded to the recent debate at Stanford and other universities over core curriculum and observed that, as a Jew, I am wedded to a highly traditional identity; much of what is most precious to me in life is found in a book, one book, the Torah. It is obvious to me that not all texts are of equal value—and not all studies as important as the careful reading of texts. On the other hand, the core curriculum I value so much, and have fought to retain with minor emendations, has rarely included books by Jews, unless you count Moses (whose presence I value) and Marx or Freud (who should not count as Jews in this connection). I have made room in my soul for a culture that has generally had no place for my people. Plato and his heirs are etched into the face I hold up to the mirror each day, though most of those authors never looked my ancestors in the eye.

It therefore does not take a lot of empathy for an American Jew to identify with other minority students and faculty distressed because they too have been omitted from the core, and until very recently could not find a single course in the university bulletin which charted the experience of their parents and grandparents on these shores. Their cause is my cause. And yet, precisely because of the history of Jews in America and our people's far longer history in less hospitable corners of dispersion, I cannot but remain committed to the construction of a common (and inclusive) American culture. Without it, I fear, we will not long hold together as a society in pursuit of liberty and justice for all—and Jews will not long have a place in America's midst.

Jews are no less in the middle when it comes to our ethnic and religious identity in American society: increasingly seen as part of "the establishment" by groups demanding as much of a place at the center as we have won, but still regarded with suspicion by some older members of the "gentlemen's club" and as objects of conversion by those who preach the virtues of Christian America. We worry, not without cause, that our achievement—a bare half century since Auschwitz, and with admission to the country clubs and boardrooms of corporations still more recent—is fragile and tenuous at best. How can one not identify as a Jew with the cause of change, the opening of every door? I have been insulted more than once by my people's exclusion from opportunity, as from the canon. But how can I not resist the deconstruction of all norms, the leveling of all hierarchies, the attempt to eliminate all centers in the name of equality and difference? I am a Jew, after all: obligated by a text, an ethical tradition, a history, the one God.

The lesson to be learned from the Jewish situation—and taught—in multicultural America, it seems to me, is that Jewish interests and Jewish principles do not always lie on one side or the other of the middle ground we occupy. Alliances, now as ever, political as well as cultural, are shifting things, born of the moment. They will vary depending on which goal is being sought at the moment, which good is being defended. Life as a minority involves perpetual and precarious balancing. We have long experience at this. It is a given in the world of Adam the first. The multicultural moment is but one more instance in an unending series.

Jewish education in this situation needs to prepare Jews for their own otherness, as Soloveitchik warned—but also for the context of multiple otherness so crucial to this culture and society. Students need to hear that pluralism inside the Jewish world, as outside it, is a blessing and not only a curse, an end and not only a means, an opportunity and not only an impediment. This too is a sort of learning for which our tradition does not prepare us: one further proof that living Torah requires tools which the Torah itself could not and did not provide.

Conclusion: The Story Continues

Jewish tradition does not allow for endings—does not much believe in them, one might say. Maimonides went out of his way to emphasize that even after the Messiah's coming, the world would continue to take its natural course. This is all the more true now, before the messianic era: whenever a reading from the prophets in the synagogue concludes on an unhappy note, one goes back and repeats a preceding verse, lest the hope needed to go forward be threatened. And every year, when one completes the reading of Deuteronomy and Torah with mention of "the great might and awesome power that Moses displayed before all Israel," one pauses briefly to say "be strong, be strong, and we will be strengthened"—and immediately begins again at the Beginning, with chapter 1, verse 1 of Genesis. The most potent display of Moses' "great might and awesome power" is our resolve to tell his story again and again—and to *add* to it, thirty-some centuries later, by living our lives in the framework which it established.

The Jewish community *can do this* in late-twentieth-century America. Reports of American Jewry's demise are premature. Predictions of our inevitable failure are unwarranted. There are, it is true, formidable obstacles standing in the way of any attempt at substantive community or ultimate commitment in contemporary America. We should not minimize these obstacles. I have tried to give them their due. But neither should we underestimate the immense resources at the disposal of American Jews—resources which include, but go far beyond, the institutional infrastructure constructed in recent decades and the unparalleled wealth already being poured into the effort of communal renewal. Our greatest resources, one cannot repeat often enough, are the tradition and the community themselves.

American Jews in this generation have renewed access to a tradition of Torah second to none in its intellectual reach and ethical power—a set of texts and commentaries which appeal to contemporary minds and hearts because of the profundity and the variety of voices that they contain and so encourage. The encounter with this tradition not only permits but demands that both mind and heart be active in taking it on, making it live. Intellectual integrity is not merely accepted but required. The self is challenged in the process, and transformed.

No less important, Jewish communities all across America, even as presently constituted, are in many cases equipped to satisfy Jews' hunger for ties that bind, providing connections that are all the more precious in a mobile and individualist society where roots are generally sought far more than they actually anchor. Whatever else Jewish involvement does for American Jews, it lets them know they are not alone in this world. There are people they can depend on, rituals that invite their performance with a full heart. And there is a project they can join, ongoing for some three millennia now, that aims at nothing less than the building of just social orders, the perfection of the world.

There is no reason why hundreds of thousands more American Jews cannot be provided in coming decades with ultimate meaning and palpable community of a sort they cannot easily find anywhere else. American Jewish institutions at their best already offer these, and offer them together; when they do, moreover, American Jews respond with great enthusiasm. Adult education programs are flourishing. Jewish Studies programs, greatly expanded in recent decades, are still growing. Day schools are springing up so fast there is a shortage of curricula and personnel. Jewish artists are engaged in a renewed dialogue with tradition that is finding its expression in an outpouring of paintings and poetry, sculpture and film. "Missions" to Israel continue to elicit Jewish identification, despite and because of the problems encountered there. Signs of vitality are abundant— even if, among a large number of American Jews, apathy and alienation remain the rule.

We can never entirely overcome the latter. Social and cultural forces are against us; ambivalence to the tradition of parents and ancestors is profound; "quality control" in synagogues, schools, and organizations will always be less than optimal; some rabbis and communal leaders will continue to preach a message of guilt and apology instead of offering positive experiences that excite minds and stir emotions. Overambitious expectations should be curbed, lest failure to achieve them inhibit the progress which can be made. But it is not at all unrealistic to believe that we can involve far more Jews than at present in the life of the tradition and community. Moving 10 percent over the next decade or two toward greater participation— half a million souls—would make an incalculable difference to the community as to them. To do so, we will have to build communities which more adequately meet the needs of those who join them, and transmit a tradition which speaks more convincingly than at present to the minds Jews bring to the texts and the lives they lead: a Torah put back in touch with the arts, sciences, and professions where the most pressing current dilemmas are confronted and will have to be overcome.

This is of course an ambitious program. It must be, to be true to Torah. But it is not entirely unrealizable. The work is ours to *do*, as the rabbis put it, and not to complete; the story demands to be told and to be lived; it by definition knows of no end. Provision of Jewish meaning in just and caring Jewish communities is the vocation which Jews have been pursuing in their generations for millennia. Our generation is called to this work in America right now, and only we can perform it. Now as ever, the work is well worthy of a lifetime and constitutes its own reward: the love and excitement which come of taking hold of Torah and making it our own; the joy of passing Torah on to others, enriched by our having lived in its embrace.

NOTES

Introduction

1. Robert N. Bellah et al., *Habits of the Heart: Individualism and Commitment in American Life* (New York: Harper and Row, 1985).

2. On the population survey of American Jewry and its implications, see the special issue "Seizing the Challenge of the 1990 National Jewish Population Survey," *Journal of Jewish Communal Service* 68:4 (Summer 1992). For analysis of the varying degrees of activism, passivity, and alienation among American Jews, see Steven M. Cohen, "Jewish Continuity over Judaic Content: The Moderately Affiliated American Jew," in *The Americanization of the Jews*, ed. Robert Seltzer and Norman J. Cohen (New York: New York University Press, 1995), pp. 395–416.

1. Genesis

1. The classic statement of this transformation remains Jacob Katz, *Out of the Ghetto: The Social Background of Jewish Emancipation, 1770–1870* (New York: Schocken, 1978).

2. A convenient, if incomplete, edition is Solomon Maimon, *An Autobiography*, ed. Moses Hadas (New York: Schocken, 1967).

3. Max Weber, "Science as a Vocation," in *From Max Weber*, ed. Hans Gerth and C. Wright Mills (New York: Oxford University Press, 1969), p. 139.

4. Max Weber, "Politics as a Vocation," in *From Max Weber*, pp. 78–79.

5. The essay is conveniently available in Immanuel Kant, *Foundations of the Metaphysics of Morals* and *What Is Enlightenment?* ed. Lewis White Beck (Indianapolis: Bobbs-Merrill, 1976), pp. 85–92.

6. Lionel Trilling, *Sincerity and Authenticity* (Cambridge: Harvard University Press, 1972); Peter L. Berger, *The Heretical Imperative* (Garden City: Doubleday, 1980).

7. Quoted in Richard Reeves, *American Journey* (New York: Simon and Schuster, 1982), pp. 197–98.

8. Abraham Heschel, *God in Search of Man* (New York: Farrar, Straus and Giroux, 1996), p. 3.

9. Matthew Arnold, "The Scholar Gipsy," in *The Penguin Book of English Verse*, ed. John Hayward (Harmondsworth: Penguin, 1970), pp. 346–52.

10. Martin Buber, "The Man of Today and the Jewish Bible," in *Israel and the World: Essays in a Time of Crisis* (New York: Schocken, 1978), p. 93.

11. I have addressed this theme in greater detail in my book *Galut: Modern Jewish Reflection on Homelessness and Homecoming* (Bloomington: Indiana University Press, 1986), pp. 3–18.

12. The essay is conveniently available as Franz Rosenzweig, "Teaching and Law," in *Franz Rosenzweig: His Life and Thought,* ed. Nahum N. Glatzer (New York: Schocken, 1976), pp. 234–42.

13. Gershom Scholem, "Revelation and Tradition as Religious Categories in Judaism," in *The Messianic Idea in Judaism* (New York: Schocken, 1974), pp. 283, 291–92.

14. See for example the methodological reflections in Judith Plaskow, *Standing Again at Sinai: Judaism from a Feminist Perspective* (San Francisco: Harper and Row, 1990), 1–24. A concise statement is available in Judith Plaskow, "Standing Again at Sinai," in *Tikkun* 1:2 (1989): 28–34.

2. Exodus

1. Friedrich Nietzsche, *On the Genealogy of Morals,* trans. Walter Kaufmann (New York: Vintage, 1969), II:2, p. 59.

2. Joseph B. Soloveitchik, "Kol Dodi Dofek: It Is the Voice of My Beloved that Knocketh," in *Theological and Halakhic Perspectives: Reflections on the Holocaust,* ed. Bernhard Rosenberg and Fred Heuman (Hoboken: Ktav, 1992), pp. 51–58.

3. Michael J. Sandel, *Liberalism and the Limits of Justice* (Cambridge, England: Cambridge University Press, 1982), p. 179.

4. Jerusalem Talmud, Tractate Hagigah, 1:7.

5. Abraham Heschel, *Man Is Not Alone* (New York: Farrar, Straus and Giroux, 1995), p. 71.

6. Friedrich Nietzsche, *The Gay Science,* trans. Walter Kaufmann (New York: Vintage, 1974), I: 26, p. 100.

7. Heschel, *Man Is Not Alone,* p. 8.

8. Moses Maimonides, "[Commentary on] Helek: Sanhedrin, Chapter Ten," in *A Maimonides Reader,* ed. Isadore Twersky (New York: Behrman House, 1972), pp. 401–23.

9. Abraham Heschel, *Torah Min Ha-shamayim* (English title: *Theology of Ancient Judaism*), 3 vols. (London: Soncino, 1962, 1965, 1990).

10. Charles Taylor, *Sources of the Self: The Making of Modern Identity* (Cambridge: Harvard University Press, 1989); Alasdair MacIntyre, *After Virtue* (Notre Dame: University of Notre Dame Press, 1981).

11. Heschel, *Man Is Not Alone,* p. 78.

12. Buber, "Man of Today and the Jewish Bible," pp. 97–98. See also Martin Buber, *I and Thou,* trans. Walter Kaufmann (New York: Scribner's, 1970), particularly part three.

3. Leviticus

1. For a comprehensive introduction to the book, see Jacob Milgrom's incomparable commentary in the Anchor Bible series, *Leviticus:1–16* (New

York: Doubleday, 1991). On purity and pollution, see the classic anthropological account by Mary Douglas, *Purity and Danger* (New York: Praeger, 1966). My own readings of Leviticus depart somewhat from both interpretations.

2. Mary Douglas makes a similar point in her *Natural Symbols: Explorations in Cosmology* (New York: Pantheon, 1982), pp. 1–18, as she tries to account for and critique the modern move "away from ritual."

3. Cf. Michael Wyschogrod, *The Body of Faith: Judaism as Corporeal Election* (New York: Seabury, 1983), pp. 17–21.

4. See Debra Orenstein, *Lifecycles: Jewish Women on Life Passages and Personal Milestones* (Woodstock: Jewish Lights, 1994).

5. Bellah, *Habits of the Heart*, pp. 20–21. An earlier version of this section of my essay appeared as "Reimagining Jewish Community in America," in *The Reconstructionist* 60:1 (Spring 1995): 5–13. The material is used with permission. Several of the points made here appeared earlier in "Theology and Community," in *Imagining the Jewish Future,* ed. David Teutsch (Albany: SUNY Press, 1992). They are reprinted here with permission.

6. Herbert Gans, *Middle American Individualism* (New York: Oxford University Press, 1988).

7. Michael Walzer, "The Communitarian Critique of Liberalism," in *Political Theory* 18 (February 1990): 6–23.

8. "Community," in *Encyclopedia Judaica* (Jerusalem: Keter, 1971), vol. 5, col. 808–29.

9. A great deal of attention has turned to synagogue decline and revival in recent years. For membership and attendance statistics, see Jack Wertheimer, *A People Divided: Judaism in Contemporary America* (New York: Basic, 1993), pp. 47–48. On the institution's problems and prospects, see Jack Wertheimer, *The American Synagogue: A Sanctuary Transformed* (Hanover: Brandeis University Press, 1987), and, on one denomination's situation, Jack Wertheimer, ed., "Conservative Synagogues and Their Members: Highlights of the North American Survey of 1995–96" (New York: Jewish Theological Seminary, 1996).

10. See the classic statement in Mordecai M. Kaplan, *Judaism as a Civilization* (Philadelphia: Jewish Publication Society, 1994), and the later, and more concise, vision of Jewish community in Mordecai M. Kaplan, *A New Zionism* (New York: Herzl, 1959), pp. 125–26.

11. The pre-eminent philosophical discussion of love in the corpus of modern Jewish thought draws on the Song of Songs to great effect. See Franz Rosenzweig, *The Star of Redemption,* trans. William W. Hallo (Boston: Beacon, 1972), part two.

12. Plato, *Symposium,* trans. Alexander Nehamas and Paul Woodruff (Indianapolis: Hackett, 1989), 206A, p. 52; compare the translation by W. H. D. Rouse in *Great Dialogues of Plato* (New York: New American Library, 1962), p. 101.

13. Martin Buber, *Good and Evil* (New York: Scribner's, 1953).

14. Buber, *I and Thou,* pp. 123–31.

4. Numbers

1. The most valuable commentary on Numbers that I know is Jacob Milgrom, *The JPS Torah Commentary: Numbers* (Philadelphia: Jewish Publication Society, 1990).

2. The terms are adapted from their use by Allan Silver in "Are Normal Politics Possible for Jews?" and "Political Agency in Jewish Thought: Biblical Kingship, Diaspora, Israel." Both manuscripts are unpublished. The political scientist Daniel Elazar has long worked toward a modern Jewish political theory framed in terms of covenant. See for example his recent book, *Covenant and Polity in Biblical Israel* (New Brunswick: Transaction, 1995).

3. Michael Walzer, *Spheres of Justice: A Defense of Pluralism and Equality* (New York: Basic, 1983), p. 31.

4. Reinhold Niebuhr, *Moral Man and Immoral Society* (New York: Scribner's, 1952), p. xii. See also Abraham Heschel's "A Hebrew Evaluation of Reinhold Niebuhr," in *Reinhold Niebuhr: His Religious, Social and Political Thought,* ed. Charles W. Kegley (New York: Pilgrim, 1952), pp. 468–86. Heschel's views closely resemble both Niebuhr's and those expressed in this essay.

5. Philip Rieff, *Fellow Teachers* (New York: Dell, 1972), p. 112. I have been unable to track down the source of the exact quotation; this passage is close.

6. On the insufficiencies of the Zionist critique, see Ismar Schorsch, "On the History of Political Judgment of the Jew" (New York: Leo Baeck Institute, 1977) and David Biale, *Power and Powerlessness in Jewish History* (New York: Schocken, 1986).

7. Martin Buber, "Hebrew Humanism," in *Israel and the World,* pp. 240–52. Quotation on pp. 246–47.

8. Max Weber, "Politics as a Vocation," pp. 77–78.

9. Cf. E. J. Dionne, Jr., *Why Americans Hate Politics* (New York: Simon and Schuster, 1991).

5. Deuteronomy

1. Ernest Becker, *The Denial of Death* (New York: Free Press, 1973). For an elegant statement of the reciprocal conferring of dignity, see Erving Goffman, "The Nature of Deference and Demeanor," in *Interaction Ritual* (New York: Pantheon, 1982), pp. 47–95.

2. Saul Bellow, *Humboldt's Gift* (New York: Viking, 1975), pp. 70–71, 264.

3. Bellow, *Humboldt's Gift,* p. 357.

4. An earlier version of this section was delivered at a conference in May 1996 on "Jewish Schooling and the Jewish Future" sponsored by the Rhea

Hirsch School of Education of Hebrew Union College–Jewish Institute of Religion.

For a fine statement that includes concrete matters omitted in the present essay, see Isa Aron, Sara Lee, and Seymour Rossel, eds., *A Congregation of Learners* (New York: UAHC Press, 1995).

5. Moses Mendelssohn, *Jerusalem,* trans. Allen Arkush (Hanover: Brandeis University Press, 1983), pp. 103–104.

6. Ibid., p. 103.

7. Ibid., p. 119.

8. Rosenzweig, "Teaching and Law," p. 238.

9. Franz Rosenzweig, "On Jewish Learning," in *Rosenzweig: Life and Thought,* p. 231.

10. Buber, "Hebrew Humanism," p. 246.

11. Martin Buber, "Education," in *Between Man and Man,* ed. Maurice Friedman (New York: Macmillan, 1971).

12. Martin Buber, "The Education of Character," in *Between Man and Man,* p. 106.

13. Buber, "Education of Character," pp. 104, 116.

14. Mordecai M. Kaplan, *The Future of the American Jew* (New York: Reconstructionist, 1967), pp. 439–40.

15. Kaplan, "Future of the American Jew," p. 445.

16. Abraham Heschel, "The Individual Jew and His Obligations," in *The Insecurity of Freedom* (Philadelphia: Jewish Publication Society, 1966), pp. 190–93.

17. Abraham Heschel, "Jewish Education," in *Insecurity,* p. 226.

18. Heschel, "Jewish Education," p. 230.

19. Joseph Soloveitchik, *The Lonely Man of Faith* (New York: Doubleday, 1992), p. 106.

ACKNOWLEDGMENTS

This book is dedicated to my friends, all of whom—in the spirit and often the letter of Pirke Avot 6:3—have taught me a great deal of Torah. They constituted the audience I had in mind when I first began to write the book as self-therapy on the occasion of turning forty; two deserve special thanks for allowing me to quote their letters (anonymously, at my insistence) in the section of chapter 5 devoted to reflection on "adulthood as a vocation." All have left their mark on me, and so on this very personal essay, in ways that I can never manage to express—though as they well know, I will never cease trying.

I particularly want to thank those who read and commented on the manuscript in whole or in part: Alice Bach, Michael Bennick, Ari Elon, Jonathan Friedan, Lawrence Hoffman, David Lindy, Russell Lundholm, Frankie Nakdimon, Nessa Rapoport, Michael Rosenak, Ted Solotaroff, Michael Strassfeld, Sharon Strassfeld, and Ellen Umansky.

Steven Zipperstein and my other colleagues in Jewish Studies at Stanford listened to an earlier draft of chapter 1, and, as usual, responded with encouragement and suggestions for which I remain grateful. Alvin Rosenfeld and his colleagues in the Jewish Studies program at Indiana University made completion of the book possible by inviting me to give portions of it as the Schwartz lectures for 1996, and then made the book better by their helpful words and unequaled hospitality during my visit to Bloomington. Janet Rabinowitch likewise offered sage advice and firm support throughout, immeasurably speeding the manuscript on its way from my desk to its readers. I am grateful to all of them for their unfailing generosity. I also thank the Reconstructionist Rabbinical College and David Teutsch for permission to use material on community originally published in *The Reconstructionist* (Spring 1995); and the Rhea Hirsch School of Education of Hebrew Union College–Jewish Institution of Religion and its dean, Sara Lee, for permission to use material on Jewish education originally presented at a colloquium sponsored by the School in spring 1996 and published this year among its proceedings.

Finally, my parents, Alan and Pearl Eisen, not only read extended portions of the manuscript but generously agreed to allow me to reflect publicly on my debt to them in the Genesis section. My wife, Adriane Leveen, worked through major sections with me and offered invaluable criticism. All three of course have worked through much else with me as well over the years—and offered still more major criticism. These are gifts which can never be repaid, but one wishes to acknowledge them nonetheless. I do so gladly here—and hope that, again in keeping with Pirke Avot 6:3, this book can be considered repayment of all I owe.

INDEX

Aaron, 76–77
Abraham, 3, 24, 25–26, 57
Adam and Eve, 24
Ahad Ha'am, 9
Akiba, Rabbi, 30, 59, 68–70, 90
Alcibiades, 103
American Jewish Committee, 22, 93, 99
American Jews: and continuity, 140–41; mobility of, 86, 92; normalcy experienced by, 21, 110, 119, 132; Otherness experienced by, 166–69; and politics, 109, 131–38; relation of Israel to, 42, 44, 123–24, 163–64; secular choices available to, 6–7. *See also* Community, Jewish
Assimilation, 6
Atonement, symbolic, 76
Authenticity, 150–53
Avihu, 115

Becker, Ernest, 152
Bellah, Robert, ix, 12, 86, 91
Bellow, Saul, 154, 155
Ben Gurion, David, 122
Berger, Peter, 11, 37
Buber, Martin, 10, 17, 52; on desire for and toward the good, 104; on the experience at Sinai, 61; God pictured in personal terms by, 60–61; on I-Thou experiences, 61, 105, 106; on Jewish education, 160–62; on the problem of modernity and faith, 22–23; ritual disdained by, 28, 106; his standard of responsibility for Israel, 127–29

Cain, 24
Caleb, 115–16

Canon, Western, 135, 168
"Cardozo" societies, 99
Census of Israel, 111
Charity, 90, 136
Children: God's presence in the birth of, 52. *See also* Parenting
Children of Noah, 120
Cholent Society (Oxford), 19–20
Chosenness, Jewish, 5
Cohen, Hermann, 60
Commitment to Judaism, 2–4, 28; as a choice, 6–7, 157; and collective history, 36; commitment to God in, 36–38; and historical consciousness, 9–10; and personal biography, 35–36; and scientific consciousness, 8–9. *See also* Covenant
Community, Jewish, ix–xiii, 85–87; boundaries of, 89–91; dissolution of, x, 173n1(1); Emancipation and the fragmentation of, 5–6; in England, 20–21; global level of, 96–98; "God-wrestling" in, 38; local face-to-face level of, 95–96; love in, 100–106; "middle-range" level of, 98–99; mobility in, 86, 92; modern individualism in, 11–14; multiplicity of affiliations in, 73, 92–93; obligation in, 38, 50; parallels in Jewish history to, 87–88; of Philadelphia, 15–18; as pluralist, 73, 93–94, 157; political community in, 111; quality vs. quantity of investment in, 92–93; revitalization of, 28, 31–32, 38, 73, 100, 170–72; ritual as source of, 81–82; self-contained period of, 4–5; symbolized in ritual, 71–72; Torah as grand narrative of, 21–22; as voluntary, 73, 91–92, 157

183

184

INDEX

186
INDEX

ARNOLD M. EISEN is Professor and Chair of Religious Studies at Stanford University, a frequent speaker on issues related to contemporary Jewish life before lay and scholarly audiences throughout North America, and an active participant in communal discussions concerning the future of American Judaism. Before joining the faculty at Stanford in 1986 he held appointments at Tel Aviv and Columbia universities. He is the author of *The Chosen People in America* (1983), *Galut: Modern Jewish Reflection on Homelessness and Homecoming* (1986), and *Rethinking Modern Judaism: Ritual, Commandment, Community* (forthcoming, 1998).